Only One Life

'How God used Zach Bertsch's Life, Cancer and Death to Save Children in Haiti'

A Biography of Zach Bertsch

by

Ed Schwartz

First Edition - 2020

OAK CREEK
media

Bluffton, Indiana

ISBN: 978-1-7336505-4-0

Chapter 1

UNUSUAL? Yes! Zach Bertsch was unusual. Anyone who knew him would quickly agree. But, then again, so were Henry Ford, Voltaire, Ben Franklin and Nikola Tesla.

For instance, Henry enjoyed eating sandwiches made of common road-side weeds between slices of soybean bread.

Voltaire had a habit of daily drinking forty to fifty cups of coffee, in spite of his doctor's warnings.

Ben Franklin reportedly made a practice of working each morning for one or two hours in his office, without clothing, with cold air blowing through the open windows.

Nikola Tesla, a genius in the electrical field, would flex his toes one-hundred times, each night, before bedtime.

We could, with some accuracy, assume that none of Henry's, Voltaire's, Ben's or Nikolas' quirks directly contributed to their personal success stories.

But, often, when we get a glimpse into the lives of 'unusual' people, we find circumstances, relationships and habits which have directly contributed to the persons' uniqueness and success. The same would be true of Zachary L. Bertsch.

Who was he?
What factors contributed to his 'success'?
Were there coincidental things which shaped his life?
What role did God play in Zach's life?
What was Zach's legacy?

Zach had many principles in life, but there were four which this book will explore. He strongly believed:

- God gave him attributes, gifts and talents which were not to be wasted.

- God gave him opportunities to serve in His Kingdom and he needed to pursue them.
- Man isn't capable of doing God's will without Christ.
- When something is accomplished, God must receive all the praise, honor and glory.

Zach would have been adamantly opposed to a biography written to bring honor to himself. But, if it could be used for God's glory, to enhance God's Kingdom, or to expose people to God, then he would have enthusiastically conceded and said with his cackling giggle, 'Let's do it'!

Zach strongly believed God placed huge potential in every human being. Often it remains dormant until we give God our 'permission' to do with us as He chooses. Then, God has His ultimate way. The results are remarkable when we watch God do His work within a willing servant.

Zach would be incredibly pleased to know his short life, decimated by cancer, could inspire others to allow God to do extraordinary things with their ordinary lives.

Many people look for life accomplishments and successes to define their legacy. Zach's legacy wasn't about his personality, spiritual gifts or accomplishments. His was a Godly legacy clearly defined by something he quoted often...

Only one life, 'twill soon be past,
Only what's done For Christ will last. - C.T. Studd

This book isn't just a biography of Zach's life. Chapters Two and Three will explore the lives of various individuals as we unpack their distinctive traits and characteristics and see what history reveals.

Chapter Four will bring God into the 'success equation' as we begin to see how He used Zach's background, personality, talents and gifts for His eternal purposes.

Chapter 2

Ancient Egypt – ca. 1750 BC

JOSEPH stood in front of his treacherous brothers with an opportunity to finally impart justice and revenge. He had absolute authority to do with them as he saw fit.

The brothers were afraid. Deathly afraid in fact. They said, "Joseph will peradventure hate us, and will certainly requite us all the evil which we did unto him."

Most certainly, the older brothers had maliciously and cruelly heaped evil upon their young brother. They had conspired to kill him due to their jealousy. Finally, one brother interceded and they instead chose to throw him into a pit in the desert. A group of merchant slave-traders passed by on their way to Egypt, so instead of leaving Joseph to die in the pit, the brothers sold Joseph to them.

What followed was an extraordinary story of grace, mercy and redemption. As second-in-command in Egypt, Joseph did an astonishing thing as his brothers stood before him. He forgave them and said one of the most profound things ever recorded. "But as for you, ye thought evil against me; but God meant it unto good, to bring to pass, as it is this day, to save much people alive. Now therefore fear ye not: I will nourish you, and your little ones. And he comforted them, and spake kindly unto them." – Genesis 50:20-21

~~~~~~~~~~~~

Ancient Persia – ca. 486 BC

ESTHER'S mother and father died and she was trafficked along with others to Persia. She was now an orphan in a new and hostile land. Life likely couldn't have taken a more drastic turn for such a vulnerable young girl. Whatever her path would have been in her native country simply wasn't to be.

The King of Persia began his search among the young women in his country for a candidate to replace his independent and nonsubmissive wife Queen Vashti. Esther, along with other young girls were groomed for the potential position. She became the chosen one, the Queen of Persia.

Is spite of the tragedies which uprooted her from her native land, the loss of her parents, being placed in slavery, Esther was now in a position to intercede for her native people, the Jews. Though conspiracies and deceptions were carried out to pit the King against her people, she as Queen put herself in harm's way to save them.

Through a series of events, she became the savior of those who had been trafficked and enslaved alongside her in Persia.

~~~~~~~~~~

Southeast Ohio – April 1968.

SHE slowly moved through the dense hardwood forest bordering the Ohio River. As was her habit, she stopped for fifteen seconds under a few maple trees and raised her head slightly to catch scents carried on the night breeze. Over her seven years as a Whitetail doe she'd learned many things necessary to survive.

Her normal pattern was to doze sporadically during the night. In the last hour before dawn she began her trek to the best grazing in the northwest. Not detecting any threats in the westerly drafts of wind, she began moving forward.

Over the last five years, she'd given birth to five sets of twin fawns, but now she was past her prime. The harsh Ohio River Valley winters, the births and the constant need to stay vigilant was taking its toll. She was stopping more often and for longer periods of time.

She raised her nose into the westerly breeze once again. She listened intently and then after ten seconds gently dropped her tired body onto the leaf covered forest floor. It was there in that spot, on that early spring day, she died a natural death. Her transition from life to forest compost began immediately.

One month later the Ohio red maples began developing their seeds. Known as a samara, the red maple seed had a pair of one inch wings attached to it. When the time was right, the seed with the dual helicopter rotors began its slow descent to the forest floor. Fluttering gently in the breeze, it blew wherever the wind randomly took it. One of those samaras landed directly on the spot where the elderly doe had given her body to the forest soil.

The samara rotors landed first, caught by blades of grass, and the seed was perched precariously and unproductively an inch above the rich dirt.

The next day, a bobcat began sniffing the ground where the doe had died a month earlier. The forty pound male stepped on the samara. The rotors broke off and the seed, under the weight of the bobcat, was embedded a quarter inch into the rich and soft soil. Finding nothing to eat he moved on, but the seed began to take root.

The rains came and went as did the four seasons for southeastern Ohio. The samara began its growth as a seedling and rapidly became a tree. The doe had provided rich and fertile soil for the tree to grow.

47 years later

"Look at that, will ya?"

Bob looked at what Pete was pointing to and said, "What?"

"We're surrounded by red maples and they're all the same height, except for this one."

Bob glanced up and around and said, "So what? That's no big deal. We see that kind of stuff all the time. You can't be a logger for forty years and not notice."

Pete replied, "Yeah, I know. But it just seems odd. Why do you suppose this one tree is so much bigger in diameter and taller than the twenty around it?"

"I don't know, maybe because it's a grandpa tree and the others are younger? Who knows and who cares. But here's something I do know. If you don't quit jawing about it, we're gonna lose our light. We need to get these trees cut. Start your saw and make some sawdust."

Howland, Maine – 1906.

PERCY, at 12 years old, slowly walked home from his grammar school, knowing his formal education had just come to a dead end. A personal tragedy was unfolding for a bright young boy. An inevitable downward spiral began. It was now time for him to get a job and add support to his family. Hiring on at a local weaving mill, he became a 'spindle boy'. For several years, the hours were long and the work was difficult, but his family needed his help. His decision to enlist in the U.S. Navy came right before WWI.

As a U.S. Navy radio operator, he had down-time. He filled those hours reading text books relating to a variety of scientific subjects and essentially became self-taught. Following his stint in the First World War, he was employed by the American Appliance Company which later became Raytheon. During World War II he was involved in the production of early radar equipment to detect the presence of German planes and submarines.

Then, in 1946, while working with a new vacuum tube and electro-magnetic waves, he noticed the chocolate bar in his shirt pocket had melted. He grabbed some popcorn kernels and held them close to the device. They popped. The patent for microwave ovens was filed and household cooking changed dramatically.

~~~~~~~~~~

In his book, *'Outliers - The Story of Success'*, Malcolm Gladwell [1] lays out the concept that 'Extraordinary achievement is less about talent than it is about opportunity'. That statement seems to contradict conventional wisdom. We naturally assume the highest IQ's and several other talent factors create the most successful people in the world.

Malcolm goes on to say, "Biologists often talk about the 'ecology' of an organism: The tallest oak in the forest is the tallest not just because it grew from the hardiest acorn; it is the tallest also because no other trees blocked its sunlight, the soil around it was deep and rich, no rabbit chewed through its bark as a sapling, and no lumberjack cut it down before it matured. We all know that successful people come from hardy seeds. But do we know enough about the sunlight that warmed them, the soil in which they put down the roots, and the rabbits and lumberjacks they were lucky enough to avoid?"

His comments were the inspiration behind my short illustration about the doe, samara, red maple tree and bobcat.

With that in mind, let's explore the foregoing four illustrations about Joseph, Esther, the red maple tree and Percy.

As we look at the life of Joseph we can discern several things.

- His father loved him more than the other brothers and gave him preferential treatment.
- The brothers in their humanness resented the favoritism.
- They entered a downward spiral of anger, bitterness and hatred leading to throwing Joseph into the desert pit and selling him into slavery.
- Joseph could have been sold by the slave-traders to almost anyone enroute to Egypt, or in Egypt, but he was sold to the captain of the Egyptian palace guards.
- That placement brought him to the attention of Pharaoh who eventually placed Joseph as second-in-command of Egypt.

Recalling again what Malcom Gladwell stated in, *'Outliers - The Story of Success'*... "Extraordinary achievement is less about talent than it is about opportunity", how do we process the life of Joseph? Are there any life circumstances Joseph orchestrated, manipulated or contrived to achieve success for himself? It seems everything we look at in Joseph's life were choices made by others which ultimately had a direct impact on him. Joseph was an ordinary man with ordinary talent, but given extraordinary opportunities.

What about Esther? Can we identify anything she had done to achieve her status as Queen of Persia and savior of her Jewish people? Let's take a look at some of her most strategic life points.

- She was born with great beauty.
- Her mother and father died when she was young.
- She was trafficked with many others into slavery in Persia.
- A relative raised her as his own daughter.
- She was selected out of many other young women to become the King's wife.
- She became a royal pawn between a bitter and violent man, intent on conspiracy; the King of Persia; and her adoptive father.

Esther's role as savior of her Jewish people is legendary. As queen she had access to the King of Persia. As we look into her life, can we find anything she planned herself?

What about the red maple tree? It, of course, had nothing to do with where the doe died. It didn't control the winds which caused the samara to land on her fertile death-bed. Nor did it control the path of the bobcat as it embedded the red maple seed into the rich soil.

Ah, then there's Percy. What contributed to his success?

- Being part of a poverty stricken family, he had to leave school at age 12.
- Just prior to WWI, he enlisted in the U.S. Navy and was given a job as a radio operator.
- With his down-time he delved into scientific books to continue his education.
- After the war he became involved with early electrical and electronic appliance manufacturing.
- When war broke out with Germany during WWII, his experience plunged him into radar production for the detection of submarines and aircraft.

- After the war, during a random test of electrical equipment, the chocolate bar in his pocket melted and the microwave was born.

Were any of those things orchestrated by him to create his own life-path and success?

As we consider the lives of Joseph, Esther, the red maple and Percy we could ask many 'what if' questions.

- What if Joseph's father had not shown favoritism among his sons?
- What if Joseph's brothers had followed through on killing their brother instead of selling him to the slave-traders?
- What if Joseph had been sold to a mason or carpenter?
- What if Esther had not been orphaned?
- What if she had not been trafficked to Persia?
- What would have happened if the bobcat had chosen another path in the forest?
- What if Percy would have spent his time reading penny-novels instead of scientific journals?
- What if Percy would have been assigned to an infantry division during WWI instead of radio operation?
- What if Percy would have had peanuts in his pocket instead of a chocolate bar?

With these illustrations, we've followed the lives of ordinary people with ordinary talents leading to extraordinary accomplishments. We've observed that none of them were self-made men or women but rather the recipients of 'opportunity'. A wide variety of non-related events or circumstances were woven together in each of the illustrations to create 'fertile soil' for extraordinary outcomes. Were they random? Were they non-related?

In the next chapter we'll follow the life of yet another man who helped change the world.

Chapter 3

Milan, Ohio ~ 1848

THOMAS was only 1 year old when he became ill. Diagnosed with Scarlet Fever, he soon developed a secondary infection which left him nearly deaf.

Upon entering public school, he was soon considered a poor student. After several months the schoolmaster dismissed him and stated that he was an 'addled child'.

Thomas' mother decided to home-school him for the next seven or eight years. During that time he developed an interest in chemistry and conducted experiments in the basement of their home in Port Huron, Michigan.

At age thirteen he started a small newspaper which he sold on trains or at the nearby train station. The profits he gained were used to purchase yet more chemical and electrical equipment for his experiments.

His hearing was further impaired due to conducting a chemical test in a boxcar. When his experiment caught on fire, he was apprehended by the train conductor who punched him on his ears and threw him and his equipment off the train.

Now completely deaf in one ear and barely hearing from the other, he learned how to 'hear' music by biting into the wood of a piano or music player so the vibrations would be registered by his inner ear.

When Thomas was fifteen, while selling newspapers at the train station, he noticed a runaway train car moving quickly down the tracks. Seeing a 3 year old boy on the tracks, he rushed to rescue him from being hit. Quickly, he became a local hero. The rescued boy's father, who was the train station agent, offered to teach telegraphy to Thomas as a reward. Eager to learn, Thomas soon mastered telegraphy and at age nineteen was hired by Western Union. He worked the night shift allowing him time to read and attempt more experiments.

One night while at work, Thomas was conducting one of his experiments on a lead acid battery and leaked sulfuric acid onto the floor. It seeped through the floorboards and onto his boss's desk below. The next morning Thomas was fired.

His next years were filled with experiments and patents for electrical equipment. Over his lifetime, Thomas Edison had 1,093 U.S. patents for a wide variety of new products which changed the world forever.

It's been said that due to his hearing loss, he worked alone which was conducive to remaining focused on what he was doing. His early failures in school created a desire to succeed and to look at life in a very optimistic way. He never looked at his failed experiments as an end result, but rather another step to yet another unforeseen, successful conclusion.

It's a simple thing to identify the 'successes' of Thomas Alva Edison as they are recorded in significant detail for the entire world to see. But, is there anything in his life he orchestrated to become the successful man he was? Was he a self-made man? Was his life defined by his own choices or by opportunities given him by others?

Again, we recall Malcolm Gladwell's statement, 'Extraordinary achievement is less about talent than it is about opportunity'.

Malcom also states in his book *'Outliers - The Story of Success'*, "I want to convince you that these kinds of personal explanations of success don't work. People don't rise from nothing. We do owe something to parentage and patronage. The people who stand before kings may look like they did it all by themselves. But in fact they are invariably the beneficiaries of hidden advantages and extraordinary opportunities and cultural legacies that allows them to learn and work hard and make sense of the world in ways others cannot. It makes a difference where and when we grew up. The culture we belong to and the legacies passed down by our forebears shape the patterns of our achievement in ways we cannot begin to imagine. It's not enough to ask what successful people are like, in other words. It's only by asking where they are from that we can unravel the logic behind who succeeds and who doesn't."

Once again we can ask the 'what if' questions regarding Thomas Edison.

- What if Thomas had not contracted Scarlet Fever and the subsequent infection which damaged his hearing?
- What if Thomas had not learned how to 'hear' music by biting the wood of a piano or music player? Did that pique his curiosity as to what else there was to learn?
- What if Thomas had gone through the public school system instead of having his mother teach him at home? Did that one-on-one focus help his learning disability?
- What if he wouldn't have saved the young boy from the runaway freight car? What if the little boy's father had given him a silver dollar as a reward instead of teaching him telegraphy?
- What if the sulfuric acid hadn't dripped onto his boss's desk at Western Union and he wouldn't have been fired? That firing pushed Thomas into his final career of self-employment and pursuit of new products and inventions.

In the next chapter we'll consider another significant reason why we can't assume our success in this world is ours to claim. The aforementioned illustrations help to explain how men and women aren't self-made, but rather recipients of others decisions and the opportunities coming their way.

Chapter 4

IN the previous chapters, we've delved into the lives of several men and women to explore if there is such a thing as a self-made person. Again and again, we find few people, if any, become successful only as a result of their own initiatives or efforts. While each of us have varying degrees of resourcefulness, intellectual capabilities, charisma and dogmatic focus, rarely will those things of themselves create success.

Rather, we've found 'opportunities' are introduced into our lives by strategic people at favorable times. Those opportunities along with our God-given gifts and talents create fertile soil for success.

There is, however, another component worthy of consideration. In fact, I've purposely held it until now, to introduce as the 'most' important factor defining 'success'. One simple word...

GOD

You may wonder why a biography of Zach Bertsch would have several chapters devoted to situations, characteristics and opportunities defining the success of other people.

It's rather simple. In our world and specifically in our western culture, huge amounts of credit and praise are heaped upon the personal successes of men and women, focusing upon 'their' efforts. Zach was successful, but he gave 'all' praise for accomplishments to God. That made him unique and unusual.

In our culture, we develop a mindset about life. It's taught by parents, teachers, churches, the sports industry, Hollywood and social media. Through those avenues we develop a concrete view about life that's difficult to change. While at times we may feel the urge to diverge from that 'typical mindset' status quo, the pressure of conventional wisdom presses in to keep us from thinking outside the box. It's much like a salmon going upstream. We believe what we believe and rarely does it change.

From the time we're toddlers, many of us are taught principles and values which create a predictable mindset:

- Hard work leads to success.
- Conservative financial practices leads to financial prosperity.
- Prayer changes things.
- The deeper our faith, the more we will see miracles in life.
- The more time we spend with our children, the more successful they will become.
- Nothing ventured, nothing gained.
- Additional education assures prosperity and success.
- The more we pour into our marriages, the stronger they'll be.

While there is certainly truth in all of the above statements, they tend to center on personal effort. More of 'this' leads to more of 'that'. Left unchecked, strong personal effort can reduce our willingness or desire to receive outside help when we're in need. In other words we can unknowingly develop a mindset of 'I can do this by myself'!

Let's look at some quotes from famous and successful people to understand what they believe leads to success.

Thomas Edison – 'Opportunity is missed by most people because it is dressed in overalls and looks like work'.

Vince Lombardi – 'The price of success is hard work, dedication to the job at hand, and the determination that whether we win or lose, we have applied the best of ourselves to the task at hand'.

Stephen King – 'Talent is cheaper than table salt. What separates the talented individual from the successful one is a lot of hard work'.

Horace – 'Life grants nothing to us mortals without hard work'.

Derek Jeter – 'When you put a lot of hard work into one goal and you achieve it, that's a really good feeling'.

Tommy Hilfiger – 'The road to success is not easy to navigate, but with hard work, drive and passion, it's possible to achieve the American Dream'.

Sandra Bullock – 'I have achieved everything through either hard work or luck'.

Colin Powell – 'A dream does not become reality through magic; it takes sweat, determination, and hard work'.

Bill Gates – 'I never took a day off in my 20's. Not one'.

Sophocles – 'Without labor, nothing prospers'.

Mark Cuban – 'It's not about money or connection – it's the willingness to outwork and outlearn everyone'.

Certainly, no one will seek to minimize the hard work, education, perseverance, blood, sweat and tears the above men and women poured into their lives to become successful. But, is there more than hard work, grit, education and perseverance to which we can attribute success? It seems the typical way in which we look at success is very 'self' driven, is it not?

But, what's missing in those famous, conventional wisdom quotes?

What other factors need to be considered?

Based on what we learned about Joseph, Esther, the red maple, Percy Spencer and Thomas Edison, we'd certainly need to add 'opportunity' to the mix. Did you notice anything in the aforementioned quotations that spoke of 'opportunity' helping to define success?

As a society we've bought into the concept of a self-made person. Unfortunately, that belief has created a number of unhealthy mind-sets in how we revere or idolize certain men and women.

The adoration and praise we as a culture heap upon movie stars, sports heroes, the very rich and political figures continues to escalate. We follow their lives and listen to their words. We revel in their activities, pay to watch them perform and dote on their personal lives. All the while, we solidify the mindset that hard work, education and perseverance leads to success.

Of course, those three commodities are clearly components of ultimate success. But are they the backbone? Are they the bedrock and foundation?

If truly the only three components of success are hard work, education and perseverance, then we would certainly and rightfully heap rewards and praise upon those who excel at all three. Their success is purely theirs to claim. They did the work and then reaped the rewards and praises of men. They are worthy of praise, are they not?

But what of opportunity in their lives? How does that component enter the equation? It's rarely mentioned, as it seemingly has little or nothing to do with the strenuous efforts put forth by the star. The reality is that opportunity comes from another source other than 'self'. It comes from without, not within, therefore either it's not recognized, simply glossed over or conveniently ignored.

Conventional wisdom would identify opportunity as luck, coincidence or chance. But is it? The atheist, agnostic or non-believer would and must call opportunity 'luck, coincidence or chance'. To call it something else would indicate there's a 'power' at play defying logic and speaks of an 'order' to things, that must be supernatural.

As Jesus followers, we quickly turn to scripture to give answers to life's questions. Since we do believe in a 'supernatural order' of things, we automatically ask, how does God fit into the equation of success?

The following verses clearly show God as the director of our paths in life. He alone is the 'power' in our lives. He specifies where we are to be at any given point in time. He is the One who created us to be who He wants us to be. He decides our personality, gifts and talents. He places us where, when and how He chooses.

1 Corinthians 12:18 - But now hath God set the members every one of them in the body, as it hath pleased him.

1 Corinthians 12:11 – But all these (gifts) worketh that one and selfsame Spirit, dividing to every man severally as (God) will(s).

Exodus 4:11 - And the Lord said unto him: Who hath made man's mouth? Or who maketh the dumb, or deaf, or the seeing, or the blind? Have not I the Lord?

James 1:17 - Every good gift and every perfect gift is from above, and cometh down from the Father of lights, with whom is no variableness, neither shadow of turning.

Proverbs 3:5-6 - Trust in the Lord with all thine heart; and lean not unto thine own understanding. In all thy ways acknowledge Him, and He shall direct thy paths.

Proverbs 19:21 - There are many devices in a man's heart; nevertheless the counsel of the Lord, that shall stand.

Romans 13:1 - Let every soul be subject unto the higher powers. For there is no power but of God: the powers that be are ordained of God.

Isaiah 42:8 – I am the Lord. That is my name and my glory will I not give to another, neither my praise to graven images.

Matthew 10:30 - But the very hairs of your head are all numbered.

Jeremiah 29:11 - For I know the thoughts that I think toward you, saith the Lord, thoughts of peace, and not of evil, to give you an expected end.

Isaiah 46:9-11 - Remember the former things of old: for I am God, and there is none else; I am God, and there is none like me. Declaring the end from the beginning, and from ancient times the things that are not yet done, saying, My counsel shall stand, and I will do all my pleasure.

As we add 'opportunity' to the success equation, it begins to take on a supernatural tone. In fact, the concept of success totally changes in context. For that we shouldn't be surprised. We've learned through life's lessons that anytime God is part of anything, things change.

According to Ephesians 3:20, when we acknowledge God, He is 'able to do exceeding abundantly above all we ask or think'. Opportunity is given by Him, to us, for His purposes.

As we consider our own lives, we come face to face with our own human weaknesses. Even our strengths have a weak side and then, all too often, we get to the end of our rope and are overwhelmed, perplexed, confused and ready to give up.

The apostle Paul spoke about how difficult life can be, but he was quick to mention that the power within us is from God -

2 Corinthians 4:7-9 - ...the excellency of the power may be of God, and not of us. We are troubled on every side, yet not distressed; we are perplexed, but not in despair; persecuted, but not forsaken; cast down, but not destroyed.

Opportunities afforded to mankind aren't rare. They happen to every man and woman, righteous or unrighteous. What makes a difference is how they are acknowledged and received by us as individuals. How quickly do we recognize opportunities as coming from God? How quickly do we thank Him for them? Do we tell others our success came as a result of an opportunity God gave us?

Often we dismiss incoming opportunities because they stretch us out of our comfort zone. We say 'no' to them due to selfishness or fear. Opportunities will ultimately go to others if we fail to receive them as a gift from God.

There's a Bible verse to consider when faced with an opportunity which may frighten us:

Philippians 4:13 - I can do all things through Christ which strengtheneth me.

It's vitally important we recognize the source of Godly opportunity. Just as important is the need to give God the glory and honor for what He accomplishes in us. When success comes, the Bible tells us what to do with it:

Revelation 4:11 - Thou art worthy, O Lord, to receive glory and honor and power: for thou hast created all things, and for thy pleasure they are and were created.

These first four chapters are purposefully written to set the backdrop for Zach's biography. This book isn't a eulogy for a man, nor a book to establish a legacy for Zach. It's a book about an imperfect man who trusted in the blood of Jesus Christ; a man who knew where his strength came from; a man quick to point to God when praise came his way; and a man who wanted everyone else to have what he had – salvation in Jesus Christ!

Many would say Zach Bertsch was a successful man. In many respects, he fit the 'success' mold almost perfectly with his passion for hard work, education, perseverance and God-given opportunity. But, I'm confident no one ever heard him take credit for any of it. Rather, he was quick to give God the glory, honor and praise for all that happened in his short life. He knew opportunities came from God. He was quick to take on those opportunities and just as quick to ask God for the strength to accomplish those tasks.

Now, let's move forward and look at what defines the true uniqueness, success and legacy of Zachary L. Bertsch.

Chapter 5

Zachary Lee Bertsch
July 25, 1982 – June 6, 2013

HOW is it possible to define the thin, tiny horizontal – between Zach's birth date and his 'Going Home' date?

11,273 days, equaling 270,552 hours. It seems like a lot of hours to fill, but Zach's wife Jenny and his children Zion and Moriah would say, 'they weren't enough'! Zach's parents, siblings and his friends would say, 'there could have been so many more'.

During Zach's abbreviated life of nearly 31 years, his heart beat one billion times, if it averaged 62 beats per minute. But anyone who knew Zach knows he wasn't average. In looking at how he lived and loved life, his heart must have beat more rapidly than most. He worked hard and he played hard. He laughed (more accurately, he cackled) hard. He competed hard. He served hard.

But for now, let's go to the beginning...

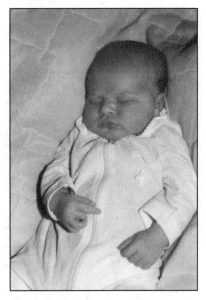

Zachary Lee Bertsch was born in Bluffton, Indiana on Sunday, July 25, 1982 to Mike and Carmon Bertsch. He was the third of Mike and Carmon's six children. Jenny, Ryan, Zach, Brad, Cassie and Danny.

Zach summed up his life this way: "I want to share with you a few memories from my past. I was the third of six children and we had a wonderful time growing up together. Ryan and I were always close and that meant that we wrestled a lot together, and I enjoyed spending time with the three 'littles': Brad, Cassie and Danny. I tried to control them with the candy club but they were uncontrollable.

"I shared a room with Brad for most of the time growing up. We had a lot of good times together too. I also enjoyed having many deep conversations with my older sister Jen, especially when I stayed overnight at her house during college.

"I am forever blessed to have a mom and dad who loved me and taught me all about life as I grew up. As a family, we went on a lot of vacations together and consequently spent a lot of time packed in a van. We loved to go to Lake Webster for a week every summer.

It became a family tradition to spend time together at Lake Webster – 2011

"My mom and dad always encouraged me to learn new things and be involved in as many activities as possible. Therefore, I was in

4-H, Boy Scouts, Business Professionals of America, Swimming and Wrestling throughout school. My mom especially encouraged me to get the Eagle Scout rank in Boy Scouts. My parents were true examples of how parents can love their children through their actions.

"I graduated high school in 2001 and then I went to college at IPFW (Indiana University and Purdue University in Fort Wayne) for a Bachelor's Degree in Accounting. I also got my Master's Degree in Business and my CPA. I really enjoyed accounting and business.

"My first big job was with County Line Swine working for Dean Gerber. I learned a lot as I worked part-time all through high school and part of college.

"Then, during college, I got an internship at International Truck and Engine and learned a lot of accounting skills there. Right after I graduated with my Bachelor's Degree, I got a good job at Lincoln Financial in Fort Wayne, Indiana doing the accounting for the broker dealer.

"After a few years I got a job at Gateway Woods Children's Home in Leo, Indiana as the business manager. I learned a lot about not-for-profit and ministry work there.

"After three years living in Leo, I applied for the job that I had been eyeing for quite a while in Bluffton, Indiana. The administrator position at Christian Care Retirement Community. I interviewed for this position and I got the job! It was shortly after this, that I was diagnosed with cancer, so I only got to work at Christian Care for a few years. I did enjoy working with the elderly and making the quality of care the best it could be.

"I'm really thankful for the years I had growing up and working. I feel like the Lord stuffed 70 years of life into 30 years because I experienced so many things, and for that I am blessed."

~~~~~~

Zach's early years were filled to the brim with family, church, education, extra-curricular activities and 'ornery' fun.

 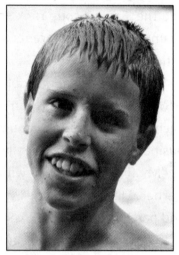

Often, as we observe adults in their vocations and life endeavors, we get a glimpse of what their childhood might have been like. Since we knew the adult Zach as someone who was full of passion, emotion, perseverance and a never-say-quit attitude, can we assume those things had their roots in childhood?

Zach's dad Mike said it this way: "Zach was a rare and unique child with a strong will. He showed that strong will even before he began walking. He was a hard child to raise because he always wanted his own way. If there were any skirmishes in the family, you knew Zach was involved. I often came home from work to find him standing in the corner for problems he'd caused."

Carmon interjects her mother's heart: "It sorta seems like we're making him sound bad."

Mike responds with a smile: "He was bad."

Zach was incredibly blessed to be part of a family which practiced unconditional love. His strong and determined spirit, though hard to manage, was nevertheless saturated with a family's love. That love created a tender heart in Zach. Carmon said, "Three things were apparent about Zach. He had a very compassionate heart, he loved babies and he was always friendly to everyone."

Older by 22 months, Ryan says of his younger brother Zach, "He was different. His speech was different and he even looked different. But, the one thing that stood out was that Zach created a crazy and wearing atmosphere for our mom and dad. Overall, he was a disaster child always needing discipline."

Trying to contain a mini-tornado like Zach was similar to herding cats. Though life was somewhat chaotic for the Mike Bertsch family, their love for Zach never wavered and somehow, someway he made his way into middle and high school.

At 4 years old, fences were probably a good idea for corralling Zach

Chapter 6

"THERE'S no way you can do it!"

Zach looked at his longtime friend Jameson Ringger and said, "You don't think so?"

"Nope. It's too far, too nasty and too dangerous for anyone to make it through."

Looking across the water of Lake Webster in northern Indiana, Zach surveyed the 50 yards of lily pads, duck weeds, black muck and likely swimming reptiles. "I can do it," he said.

Again, Jameson said, "No way anyone can get through that!"

Jameson's brother Jeremy then looked at Zach and said with a grin, "Bet you can't!"

Then the inevitable 'cackle' happened. Zach had a high pitched giggle masqueraded as a laugh that everyone said sounded more like a cackle. He said, "What'll you give me if I do it?"

By now, the Ringger boys knew what was next in their traditional game, "We'll give you a king-sized Butterfinger candy bar!"

Standing on the dock, Jameson and Jeremy watched as Zach dove into the lake and began swimming and clawing his way through the 150' of gunk.

Jeremy muttered under his breath, "Zach, you're either not very smart or you're one determined kid!"

They watched as Zach maneuvered and plowed his way through the muck to receive yet another of his most sought after treasures – a king-sized candy bar.

The Mike Bertsch and Kendall Ringger families spent a lot of time together. Vacations and Sunday suppers at Pizza Hut were prime times for the Ringger boys to egg on an all-too-willing Zach.

Jameson remembers Zach having a love for all candy, but especially king-sized Butterfinger candy bars. That 'sugar-love' created great entertainment as he knew Zach would do almost anything to get another candy bar.

"Bet you a Butterfinger you can't eat all the crushed red peppers in that jar!"

"Bet you can't eat a bowl of jalapenos without taking a drink!"

There didn't seem to be a bet Zach wouldn't rise to and 'food' ended up being the inevitable reward.

According to Kellan Kershner, another friend, "Food meant the most to Zach. Throughout our childhood, food was of high importance. This might be powdered sugar donuts, potato chips, candy, breakfast, lunch or dinner. He liked it all!"

Zach's brother Ryan shares, "He was an adventurer, quick-witted and at the same time very intelligent. He seemed to thrive on risk and adventure."

Jameson recalls their times at Lake Webster and the go-cart track at Adventure Land. "I'm not sure there was a year Zach completed the race without being black-flagged for reckless driving. It just came natural to him."

He also remembers other attributes of Zach. "He was very smart and some would say he was too smart. His smartness probably curbed his common sense.

"The lack of common sense made him super gullible. He would do and believe almost anything. Being a very good listener made it possible to feed him a line that was unbelievable and then we'd watch him suck it in."

Zach was always up for a challenge. When common sense didn't prevail, he generally paid the consequences.

Ryan remembers an incident at Gordon's Campground in northern Indiana. Jameson had a unique ability to scheme up situations to get predictable and entertaining results from Zach. In this case, he encouraged Zach to light a firecracker and throw it at another boy. Of course, Zach complied and received the predictable and anticipated results. He was caught. The other boys watched as Zach's dad Mike took him to their camper for some 'Biblical instruction' and 'unconditional love'.

Ryan says, "Though Dad and Mom provided a lot of boundaries for Zach, as well as discipline when things went wrong, Zach still did dumb and bad things.

"Numerous times he was kicked out of class, even though he was a 4.0 student with straight A's. A teacher once asked Zach, 'How can you be so smart and yet so bad'?"

Continuing, Ryan said, "I never saw him touch a book!"

It seems like a dichotomy for someone to be so bright and driven, yet have a side to them that's full of unbridled, ornery and rebellious fun. That continually got Zach into trouble.

Jim Rinkenberger, as Zach's middle school math teacher, remembers an incident.

"Zach was blessed with a tremendous zest for living which soon became evident when he was a student in my seventh grade advanced math classroom. He came to class daily with his unique personality, flavored with a subtle teasing nature, which was about to take on an added dimension. He was even called the class clown by some of his peers.

"One specific teasing incident occurred when Zach's nature took a turn from teasing to a combination of both teasing and flirting. One time, when he was working on a problem, Zach got a little rambunctious when creating his equation! One of the girls was yelling at Zach to stop marking on her arm and hand with the magic markers. He even got some marks on the blouse she was wearing. I told Zach that he had been asked by her to stop, and to consider this his warning to quit or he'd face consequences. His marker didn't stop. Thus, it was consequence time.

"After observing that most detentions were very ineffective, my system changed to giving out what I called attention time. Before the middle schoolers would be allowed into the lunch room, they had at least a ten minute wait. It was during these ten minutes that a student served his attention time in my classroom. I tried to make the punishment fit the situation. Zach's punishment? He had to carefully cut out 100 paper dolls (about two dolls per sheet of regular paper). Next, he had to colorfully mark each of the dolls with several different color markers, and he was to color them decently dressed with blouses, skirts, socks and shoes. When he was finished with each doll, almost all of the paper was colorfully covered. Then his finishing act was to wad up each paper doll and throw each one individually into a trash can which was about six feet from him. After all shots were made into the trash can, the full week attention time was over."

Jim continued, "Academically, Zach was very gifted in math, and even though he usually made an A+ on each of his tests, he would always, on each test handed back, persist in challenging each point that had reduced his score."

Jon Isch, a friend of Zach's and fellow classmate, saw that same persistence. "Zach was a good debater. He didn't like to lose. I remember multiple times when he would have one or two questions wrong on a test at school and he would challenge the teacher on why his answer wasn't correct. Sometimes, the teacher would accept Zach's answer."

Jim Rinkenberger as Zach's math teacher recalled another incident. "To get to our school, Adams Central, Zach and I traveled the same last 6 miles on SR 124. One morning, after I drove past the Bertsch home on SR 124 on my drive to school, I was surprised, when seemingly out of nowhere, a hot-rodder passed me as if I was 'standing' still. I recognized both the car and the driver. You guessed it. It was Zach.

"I still had probably three to four miles to go on SR 124 before coming to the stop sign on SR 124 at its intersection with Route 27. And guess who was still waiting at the 124 stop sign while waiting for the through traffic on 27 to thin out? Zach! I had caught up with him.

"I really felt a burden to share with Zach my concerns regarding his crazy driving that morning. So, after talking with him and taking into account that I was the father of three boys who weren't too far behind the ages of the Bertsch kids, I called Zach's dad Mike and shared my concerns regarding Zach's driving that morning. After all, I would want to know if and when our three sons drove like Zach did!"

As Mike reflects on the differences between Ryan and Zach, he remembers, "Ryan, as the older brother, often took advantage of Zach. Ryan was older, coordinated and good at sports... Zach not so much. But, Zach was superior in intellect, though always in Ryan's shadow."

Ryan agrees, "I wasn't a good influence on Zach. I encouraged him to try things and would get him into trouble. I remember giving him chewing tobacco one time and then sat back and watched as he got sick."

When you add Zach's competitiveness, gullibility, lack of common sense, spirit of adventure and risk-taking, you have the makings of disaster or fun. People, including Ryan, enjoyed putting Zach into positions of taking the fall.

One afternoon when school was over for the day, Zach and Ryan were driving the six miles to their home. Ryan remembers, "Zach was driving and I was riding shotgun. We were in Zach's dark navy, 4 cylinder, 5-speed Ford Mustang when we came up behind an old, beat-up, farm pick-up truck travelling slowly. I said, 'Zach, pass this old truck'. As Zach was going around the truck I leaned over and honked the horn. Zach said, 'Ryan, why did you do that'? I just laughed as yet again, Zach had to take the blame.

"Shortly after we passed the truck, we had to slow down for some slow traffic. That's when the farm truck passed Zach. It went around Zach's Mustang and came to a screeching halt on the highway, forcing Zach to stop quickly. As soon as the truck stopped, the driver's door opened and out stepped a three hundred pound farmer! His face was red with anger. He came back to our car and began to yell at Zach about his inappropriate driving. He even punched Zach's window. Zach was terrified that his window would break. The man finally stopped yelling and went back to his truck. As Zach started to drive away, I leaned over and honked the horn at the truck again! Again Zach said, 'Ryan, why did you do that?' And again, I just laughed."

Jon Isch, as a very close childhood and longtime friend of Zach, has many memories. "Looking back, Zach and I were very different. We were best friends through school but we were opposites. Zach was more of a risk taker. He wasn't as athletic, but he was smart and passionate enough to usually win. He was book smart, but didn't have much common sense. I had common sense, but not much book smarts. I guess opposites attract! We were a good team."

Continuing, Jon remembers, "Through our Middle School and High School years it was all about getting attention. Zach and I were in an unannounced competition of doing or saying 'dumb' stuff in order to get attention from classmates and to try to frustrate the teacher. When we were in the same class we would say things and do things to get the class to laugh at us. The problem was that Zach didn't know when to stop. He would continue to say and do things until the teacher lost all patience with him and he would get yelled at or kicked out in the hallway.

"Even though he had a tendency of taking things too far, I was amazed how people were drawn to him because of his wit. He had a very likeable personality. He wasn't easily offended, unless it was his brothers Ryan or Brad pestering him.

"Zach never wanted to lose at a game or a debate. When it came to athletics, he wasn't the most coordinated, but again, with his strong passion and competitiveness, he usually managed to win.

"He was a minimalist when we were in school. He would only study at the last minute, or study the least amount he thought necessary and he would still get an 'A' on the test. Instead of studying, he would be working or enjoying life. Meanwhile, I would study for two hours and get a 'B' and he would study for five minutes and get an 'A'.

"In high school, Zach was successful by only taking the classes that were necessary. He didn't go over and above to achieve the highest grades or take the highest level of Calculus, simply because he wouldn't need it for his future. Instead, he took the time to work and earn money. He wasn't focused on keeping his car clean, wearing the nicest clothes or being the most popular. His decisions in life were business oriented. That was the way he was wired.

"Though he loved telling people he drove a Mustang to see their impression, he was quick to tell them it was a 4 cylinder beater car. What he drove didn't matter to Zach and he drove that car through high school and almost all the way through college. He drove it until it was ready to die. I went with him car shopping when he was ready to finally get a different car. I remember thinking that all the cars he was looking at weren't fancy or the best looking, but they were down-to-earth models. That's who Zach was.

"Zach was also resourceful and financially conservative. When we lived together during college, he would pour the left-over coffee back into the coffee-maker and brew another pot through the same coffee grounds from the day before.

"He always had to get the best deal and had a great business mind. It seemed God gave him a gift of being business-savvy. Whether it was trading candy with me at church or trading baseball or football cards at a sleep-over, he enjoyed the discussions and debates over why he wasn't getting a very good deal out of the trade.

"Though we all had fun trying to get Zach into trouble, sometimes he needed help in getting out of it. "I remember a 4-H party we were having at Pine Lake one summer day. One of the fun things to do was to jump across the 'Lily Pads' which were a series of covered tubes with a cargo net stretched over them. You would try to see how far you could go without grabbing the net. On that particular day, there was a boy who was also enjoying the Lily Pads. This kid was not taking his turn in line and instead butting in. He was also causing some disturbance on the Lily Pad tubes by pushing tubes with kids on it and causing them to go in the water.

"The bully set off Zach's temper. He and the boy began to get into a little bit of a scuffle by pushing and shoving one another. The boy went away and Zach and I kept playing. A little while later, the boy came back to the Lily Pad area and approached Zach. I remember him saying to Zach, 'My dad said I could go out in the parking lot and fight with you. Do you want to go'? It all happened so fast, but I remember Zach's first response was 'Yeah, I'll fight you'.

"At the same time that Zach was responding to the boy, I'm sizing him up against Zach. The logical response in my mind was, 'This boy is bigger, has bigger muscles, and has the drive for a fight. I don't think this is a good idea'. I was also thinking about the trouble that someone is going to get in and that made this seem like bad idea.

"Before Zach and the boy took the next step away from the Lily Pads and headed toward the parking lot, I said in a whisper to Zach, 'This isn't worth it. Come on. Let's just go over to the zip line and leave this kid alone.' I'm not sure what Zach thought or what changed his mind, but he told the kid he was going with me. We turned and walked the opposite direction away from the boy. I don't think we ever saw him again.

"Knowing Zach, if the fight would have happened, Zach probably would have gotten a bloody nose, as he did often during wrestling matches; he would have received a few bruises; and probably been grounded by Carmon. But I think he would have used his conniving (not glamorous) wrestling moves along with his drive to win, to beat that kid. However, I was glad we didn't have to go through that!"

Due to their close friendship, Zach and Jon Isch had ample opportunity to get in trouble together. Zach the leader and Jon the follower. Zach the instigator and Jon the savior. Zach the willing and

Jon the cheerleader. That relationship prompted Zach's dad Mike to say, "I often had to apologize to Jon's dad Barry, because there was no way his son would have ever gotten in trouble if it weren't for Zach."

Zach had opinions and enjoyed debating with others. Dean Gerber, who employed Zach during high school and college years at County Line Swine had one such memory.

"Once, we had a sow that came into the farrowing crate (to farrow babies) and I questioned whether or not she was pregnant. Zach said she was pregnant and I thought she was not! Sometimes we had 'false pregnant' sows, and I thought this was one of them. They look pregnant, but no babies.

"I told Zach that I didn't 'bet', but I'd give him $50 if she had babies. I was so confident it was a false pregnancy that I told him he didn't have to pay me anything if she didn't! I thought my years of experience would prove my ability to 'ultrasound with my eyes'. She had a small belly and no udder dropping down to nurse babies, so I was confident she wasn't pregnant! Finally she went well over her due date and I knew I had guessed it right! Well, not so. A few days later she delivered two babies and I delivered a $50 bill to a self-satisfied Zach."

Working at County Line Swine was a very positive experience for Zach in developing good work ethics. He commented on Dean Gerber's management style. "Dean would give responsibilities to Ryan and me and then let us make decisions. That gave us some ownership in helping with the success of his business."

One of the life-forming factors in Zach's life was his years in scouting and finally achieving Eagle Scout ranking. To become an Eagle Scout, a young man must be accomplished in camping, cooking, navigation, nature, aquatics, first aid, fitness, leadership, safety and citizenship. His passion for achieving goals served him well, as he pursued the Eagle Scout rank. But, there were still parts of Zach that continued to remain true to his personality.

18 year-old Zach at his Eagle Scout achievement celebration with his family
Only 4% of all Scouts rise to the Eagle Scout rank

Dan Kershner, as a scout leader, spent many hours and days with Zach. Meetings, as well as trips, permitted Dan some glimpses into what made Zach tick. He remembers a couple of scouting trips in particular.

"One summer we were at a scout camp named Camp Chief Little Turtle. Our troop was down at the pond fishing when it was time to leave. Zach's adult patrol leader said it took him four or five times to get Zach to quit fishing to go back to camp and prepare for the next event. Zach would say, 'I'll be right there'. 'Can we stay a little longer'? 'Just a few more minutes'. 'Can we come back later'? Sometimes, Zach taught us just how much patience we didn't have! He was a joy to be around, but he kept us on our toes.

"Another summer, we were in Canada on a 'high adventure' trip, on a lake with no one around, except the scouts and their leaders. One night after supper, Zach asked if he and another scout could go fishing in a canoe. Fishing off the shore just wasn't good enough for Zach. He was told he had to stay within sight of camp and be back before dark. Those were two simple and identifiable rules.

"They got out so far we could barely see them on the horizon. It began to get dark and finally we could see them coming to shore. But as young scouts, they had a difficult time canoeing straight. Right, then left. Finally they came back to shore just before dark. Zach was always pushing the boundaries."

Zach's younger sister Cassie has a memory of Zach that spoke of her respect for him as well as his fortitude to accomplish a goal. His scouting group was scheduled to hike the Appalachian Trail during the summer. Zach was excited to go and ready for the adventure.

Cassie recalls the time. "I remember swimming in a little pool in the yard when I was probably 10 years old. Zach came limping by with no pants and blood pouring from his knee. I just gawked at him as he staggered on by. He had stepped over a PTO shaft while working in the barn. The rotating PTO caught his pants as he stepped over it. His pants were quickly ripped off and the shaft severely gouged his knee. He went to the doctor to get repaired and received the caution to not do anything strenuous or dangerous. That, of course, didn't stop Zach. He stubbornly braved hiking the Appalachian Trail with his Boy Scout group! I knew that took some strength and endurance with or without an injury!"

Tyson Frauhiger grew up with Zach, but their friendship didn't blossom until their high school years. Tyson has fond memories of being included in the Mike Bertsch family as a result of his friendship with Zach.

He says, "There's a few things that stood out to me about the Mike Bertsch family in general. First off, they are all hilarious and will do what it takes for a good laugh, including looking stupid or making fun of themselves. They love people, food, and are all intelligent. I can back most of this up with my earliest memory of being with them.

"After our families spent an evening together at a bonfire, I was invited to spend the night at the Bertsch's, even though I barely knew them. I accepted the invitation, and I distinctly remember feeling like a bit of a celebrity.

"It was almost like a competition between Ryan, Zach, and Brad to see who could make me laugh the most or come up with something I would like to do. I was amazed by how fast they could conquer every edition Super Mario brothers ever created. They proceeded to show me shortcuts and cheat codes (which I never even knew existed) for what seemed like most of the night.

"They had a huge container, the size of a thirty gallon barrel, full of GI Joes, which they used to entertain me with a variety of comical little skits and sophisticated war plots.

"On their love for food, they were all more than willing to share from their impressive candy stashes. I was told several times about the treat that awaited me the next morning – Mike Bertsch's scrambled eggs!

"That was all in just one sleep-over. So fast forward five years or so, to when I was good friends with Zach. There were some things that stood out in their home that are worth mentioning.

"One, the brothers could be pretty demanding of each other, not so unusual I know, however it was the way they communicated the seriousness of their demands. Often times there were a number of 'punches' that accompanied the demand. For example, 'Brad! Change the channel on the TV or ten punches'! Or, 'five punches if anyone takes my seat while I get snacks'! So, the higher the number of punches, the more serious the demand. It was a pretty simple concept and seemed reasonably effective, at least for the older boys. Brad kind of got the short end of the stick, being the younger brother, but it struck me as unique to say the least.

"Two, they often had an indoor pet, again which is fairly normal. However, their pet was a snow white, red eyed, albino rat they let freely roam the house most of the time. It always made for a good laugh when the rat got to meet new people. Possibly a better way to say it would be that new people met the rat!

"Third, the Bertsch men are smart, quick, coordinated, very money conscious and competitive. I can't really say that is extremely abnormal, but it's an interesting combination that made for some stimulating moments when they developed games that required all of those attributes.

"All the Bertsch's have fast reaction time. I remember playing a game where you set a quarter in the middle of the table with someone at each end. A third party says go and you see who can get the quarter first. The competition was pretty much between the Bertsch's as no one else could compete.

"Zach was money-conscious and a debater. When you put those two things together, you never knew what could happen. I remember a time when Zach, Jon Isch, Jeremy Reinhard and I were trying to get movie tickets for free, since we didn't have enough money. After thoroughly annoying the cashier with smart remarks and pleasantries, Zach gets a more serious sly look on his face, and proceeds to get a wrinkly and crusty dollar bill out of his wallet. He took the dollar, kind of stretched it and snapped it out straight a couple of times in the cashier's line of sight and said, 'What if George Washington asked you to let us in? What would you say to that'? We were promptly removed from the premises!"

Tyson continues in his memories of Zach, "Zach was very smart. A lot of people drew conclusions about Zach because of his ability to do or say dumb things. But there was no doubt in my mind that doing or saying dumb things was a choice Zach made. He had an uncanny ability to see if it was going to be to his benefit to act one way or another. As a result, by his own choosing, he didn't always come off as the 'brightest bulb' in the package."

Jeremy Reinhard, another good friend remembers how 'hard' Zach lived life. He always had a full schedule with work, school and extra-curricular activities. "I was roommates with Zach our last year of college. True to his nature, Zach maintained a very full schedule between work, classes, Bible studies, friendships, and other outreaches. This resulted in many late nights for him, and early mornings, which often came too soon for him, and were hard for him to wake up for.

"For Christmas that year, he received two particular gifts – an alarm clock that played CD's and a music CD by *'Becky and Ronda'*. When the alarm clock went off in the morning for the first time, it would always begin with the first song on the CD. The problem was that the first song was an incredibly calming song titled *'Angels Rock Me to Sleep'*. He'd hit the snooze and again the calming song would put him back to sleep. Again and again. Needless to say, additional persuasion was required to wake him up many mornings that semester."

Zach's outgoing nature made him a relational person. He was all about 'people' rather than 'things'. That in itself could get him in trouble unwittingly. Tyson Frauhiger says of Zach's driving abilities, "He was a terrible driver. But, in my opinion, the bad driving was due to him concentrating on communicating with those in the car with him, rather than on the road."

Others help to define Zach's personality and communication skills. Jeremy Ringger says, "He had a great gift to put others at ease by cracking jokes about himself. I cannot think of a person who was 'tense' around Zach. I know he loved to make people laugh and achieve goals that many couldn't even fathom."

Jeremy Reinhard remembers, "Zach had a great ability to pull others in. Whether it was simply a group of friends or people spending time together, he seemed to make all feel included and created an atmosphere of togetherness."

He continued, "As a generality, I remember conflict resolution was something he'd prioritize when needed. He wasn't one to hold on to his own pride.

"Zach would often use stories and humor when interacting with any group of people. He seemed to be able to connect with most people and easily form friendships."

Jameson Ringger reflects, "Zach was a softy until you made him mad and he went from subtle to swinging in two seconds! But, Zach was liked by everyone because he could make you laugh just by living life."

As we consider the childhood and teenage years of Zach's life we can begin to see very specific attributes of his personality and passion.

- Living life to its fullest
- Relationship driven
- Not impacted by materialism
- Comfortable in a leadership role
- Quick to confront
- A love to debate
- Competitive
- Friendly and outgoing
- Financially conservative
- Love for family and friends

How did those characteristics impact the rest of his life? The following chapters help to define what would happen next.

Chapter 7

REPENT... It was a simple word, often heard in Zach's high school Sunday School class. It was a concept preached regularly from the pulpit of his Bluffton church. It was talked about in the Mike and Carmon Bertsch family.

Though the word is 'simple' and the definition easy to memorize, the application to one's life is much more difficult. However, the rewards are life-changing and eternal.

Acts 3:19 establishes the Biblical command – 'Repent ye therefore and be converted, that your sins may be blotted out, when the times of refreshing shall come from the presence of the Lord'.

The word 'repent' indicates a dual meaning: Feeling remorse or sorrow for sin; and to turn from evil toward good.

Another word often used in tandem with the word repent is 'conversion', indicating again, the concept of 'change'.

Confession of sin is a means by which we align ourselves with God by acknowledging and agreeing with Him as to what the specific sins are in our life.

Zach knew that none of his own personal efforts could settle the debt He owed God for his sinful life. He was adamant that the only available payment he possessed was the faith to believe that the shed blood of his Savior Jesus Christ settled the debt.

Zach's testimony of what happened on May 7, 2000 outlines his personal process of repentance, conversion and being born again.

"I am so thankful that I was born in a Christian family with a wonderful heritage. My family went to the Apostolic Christian church in Bluffton and my parents were dedicated members. We were a family that believed that Christians should choose Christ when they were of the maturity level to be able to do so of our own free will.

"Being raised in a Christian family didn't make me a Christian. As I grew up I knew that I was not automatically a Christian. I had to make a decision to serve Christ on my own. When the time came and I was convicted of my sin, I chose to walk away from the call of Christ. I was too involved with my friends and sports to serve Christ. This was a sad decision in my life and I had several years of dreaded conviction. I knew that I was going to hell if I died and my heart became harder with each passing day.

"During my junior year in high school I became extremely convicted of my sin. Because I felt that I was already going to hell if I died, I turned to more purposeful evil to hide my sin-sick soul. My brother Ryan had started repenting and was enjoying his new life in Christ. One of my good friends, Tyson Frauhiger, also started repenting and was doing more things with the church young group instead of with us. My closest friends, Jonathan Isch and Jeremy Reinhard, were equally convicted. We were a sad group of friends who were choosing wrong instead of right.

"After the wrestling season ended during my junior year, I began seriously thinking about surrendering to Christ. I became more and more miserable as I languished in the pit of sin.

"On May 7, 2000, Jonathan Isch had dropped Jeremy Reinhard off and was dropping me off at my home after we had watched a movie. As I got out of the vehicle Jonathan asked me, 'Zach, what's holding us back'? I got back in the vehicle and shut the door. It was then and there that we decided to repent of our sins and start following Christ that night.

"We called Jeremy to see if he wanted to join us. We all three went to see Ed Schwartz, our church's elder. It was there that we confessed our sins and started our walk with Christ.

"From that day forward I've never regretted this decision. It has been awesome to serve the Lord and grow spiritually. From the very beginning I had a desire for God's Word and I've always enjoyed studying the Word ever since.

"I was baptized on February 11, 2001 and was thrilled to share my testimony of faith in what God had done in my heart. God has been faithful to me during all of life's trials and decisions. I love Jesus more than anyone and I look forward to serving him for eternity."

Was there a super-natural heart-change for Zach? How did his new relationship with Christ affect his daily life?

Zach's dad Mike says it this way, "On the day Zach gave his heart to the Lord, he changed dramatically. Instead of working for himself, it became all about working for God and Zach was tenacious in that. On that day, he quit driving me crazy!"

Ryan as Zach's older brother remembers, "On May 7, 2000, Zach came to Christ and repented for his sins. He was instantly changed. There was an instant fire for Bible memorization and apologetics and for serving the Lord. He was an inspiration. He was intelligent and had answers. He had a drive for missions. There was a fire about him."

Younger sister Cassie said, "A lot of people have passion. Zach did too. What made him different was that he 'acted' on that passion. Through words and actions, he abandoned fear and reputation. A lot of people say things, but Zach lived them! His biggest success in life was Christ living through him. There was no half-hearted conversion. When he repented, he was changed from the inside out. And I noticed!

"There was a time when Zach was a Christian and I was not. He was the only brother I remember asking me directly about it. In fact, I have vivid memories of the skip in my heartbeat when he would knock on my bedroom door. I could even identify his footfall on the steps coming up and I always got so nervous if it was him! He wasn't afraid of my questions, or my discomfort. He knew there were more important things. I know a lot of people have said this, but, 'if it weren't for him I'm not sure where I would be'. It's just who he was.

"Zach had a cheesy grin. He was so goofy and loveable that it was easy to feel comfortable around him. I admired his keen ability to meet just anybody and instantly be talking and laughing and probably asking a serious 'Kingdom-focused' question or two in between."

Younger brother Danny says, "Zach sowed many wild oats as an unconverted person, but I think God used this to show how much of a transformation someone can have when they turn their life over to Him. After Zach became a Christian, it was amazing how different of a person he became in a short period of time. I specifically remember as a 10 year old in 1999, I was worried about Zach's salvation because I knew he wasn't ready if Jesus would come back. But a few years later, I was in the young group with him and he was a huge role model to me by that point.

"Zach had a good sense of humor, so he was a fun person to be around, but he wasn't afraid to be blunt with people and speak his opinion if he disagreed with you on something. He would often challenge people, which would make them uncomfortable, but I know for me, it helped me to be a better person."

Jon Isch began his walk with the Lord on the same evening as Zach. "That night changed the rest of our lives. Zach turned his focus and passion to soaking up the Bible. It was encouraging to grow with Zach in our spiritual walk. The 'problem' was that Zach grew spiritually by leaps and bounds and I was still taking baby steps! I was thankful to have my best friend as a spiritual rock and encourager.

"I remember one time after we began our walk with the Lord when Zach was struggling. Zach and I thought that we should go talk to our wrestling coach in person and let him know of our decision. I remember Zach saying that this was hard for him. He was quiet as we approached the school. I remember asking him why and he said that he felt like he was disappointing the coach for the next season. During our conversation with the coach, Zach choked up a little and got teary eyed as he relayed the news. The coach gave us a little bit of a fun teasing, but he was happy for the decision we made. I think Zach felt much stronger and peaceful after facing this difficult situation and talking with the coach in person. It had a more positive impact with the coach than if he would have avoided him."

Jon continues, "Zach would find a way to be sarcastic with people and get them to laugh. He used humor to initiate a relationship. He wasn't afraid to ask more difficult questions to dig deeper in those relationships."

Zach's friend Tyson Frauhiger admired his friend's depth. "From my point of view, after conversion, Zach just devoured the Word. He had an understanding of it that I envied. He would bring scripture into everyday conversation that I would have never even thought about. Half the time I would have to say, 'Oh, that's what that scripture means'?"

Jeremy Reinhard remembers those early days with Zach in their walk with the Lord. "Zach seemed to possess an unparalleled drive and consistently looked toward or created opportunities for outreach for Christ. Zach was often the initiator of bringing people together, ranging from Bible studies, potluck groups, group outreaches to simply spending time with groups of friends. He seemed to be wired to see a need; note the opportunity; and develop a plan for how to meet that need. This went for both spiritual endeavors, like pulling a few young couples together to volunteer weekly at the International House; as well as daily living, like buying a house in Fort Wayne for young men to live together while in college."

Alan Ringger of Bluffton has a passion for helping young men grow in their walk with Christ. He developed a Bible Study around the time when Zach came to Christ. "Zach was an integral part of how and why my Bible Study started. His desire to learn, fellowship and teach was evident to me and obviously to everyone who was a part of that study.

"He had so many gifts. He was wise far beyond his years. He had such a heart for others and I witnessed that when I first met him at Gordon's Campground when he was in the eighth grade. I watched him befriend a challenged classmate. He cared for people in ways that I had never seen before. His consistency was incredible to watch.

"One gift that Zach didn't have was singing. I can still hear his 'joyful noise'. He often joked about it and even embraced it."

Ron Kipfer, as a minister in Zach's Bluffton church had a passion for 'apologetics', the understanding and teaching of the reasoning and discussion points behind Biblical principles. Zach and a few others became involved with Ron in developing apologetics classes to teach others of the 'argument' points and methods surrounding 'why we believe what we believe'. Even more importantly, they taught the methods by which those principles can be effectively conveyed to others.

Ron said, "Zach was very dedicated to a cause, whatever that may be. For his adult life, one of his overriding causes was to know Jesus better and better. That desire led to a very intense Bible study process in which he studied and memorized scripture and more importantly, practiced it. He truly lived out Ezra 7:10 – 'For Ezra had prepared his heart to seek the law of the Lord, and to do it, and to teach in Israel statutes and judgments'.

"Zach told me how his dedication and drive worked against him in high school, getting him into trouble. He felt if the Lord had not gotten hold of him, that satan would have used his abilities for the wrong purposes. However, God was able to turn him around and use Zach's many talents for His glory!"

Ron remembers Zach's role in the apologetics classes. "I appreciated his role in the 'Defend the Faith' series. Zach taught a few lessons not only in Bluffton but in some of our other churches. He related to audiences very well and had much knowledge about what he was talking about."

Zach's youngest brother Danny reminisces about those days, "Zach loved to argue with people, challenge people and defend his opinions. One way he used this trait to glorify God was when he and Ryan did the 'Defend the Faith' presentations. These classes taught Christians how to stick up for their faith when encountering opposition from the world and I think they were very valuable to many people, including me."

Continuing, Ron Kipfer said, "I believe his effectiveness stemmed from his daily, intense devotional life. The founder of the Salvation Army, William Booth once stated, 'Work as if everything depended upon your work and pray as if everything depended upon your prayer.' Zach lived that out very well."

Zach had purpose in his life. One of his lifetime goals was to help others find their way to Christ, the one and only pathway to God.

Zach strongly believed and lived something Charles Spurgeon once wrote about sharing the Gospel...

"If sinners be damned, at least let them leap to hell over our bodies. If they will perish, let them perish with our arms about their knees. Let no one go there unwarned and unprayed for."

Zach wrote a poem titled 'Too Late' which characterized his own personal devotion for unbelievers.

A neighbor of mine died and went to hell.
He was sorry for his sin, I could tell.

But it was too late:
Eternity he would spend behind hell's gate.

From hell, Heaven he could see:
When he looked up, he saw me.

He thought, "I knew that man. He was nice."
I was walking through paradise.

Then about me, he started to doubt:
I had never told him what Jesus was about.

I never told him how Jesus' blood can save.
I meant to, but it was too late. He's in his grave.

A lesson has been learned from this tale:
At sharing the Gospel message, I will never fail.

I will take every chance to spread God's Word.
I will make sure everyone I know has heard.

God's Word I will openly confess,
And I will be a living witness.

Young Group Friends - 2003

College Room-mates - 2004

Chapter 8

ZACH spent his last year of high school as a new Christian believer and then graduated in the spring of 2001. His focus as a senior was diametrically opposed to his earlier years in middle school and high school. No longer was he the class clown seeking attention, he was now admired for his faith by students and faculty alike. The change in his life had been dramatic.

The next four years after graduation were spent at the Indiana University and Purdue University campus in Fort Wayne pursuing a Bachelor's Degree in Accounting.

But not all his heart was dedicated to education and his future vocation. Jenny Rufener was now on his radar screen.

"So, tell me about your job with the kids at Gateway Woods", Zach said to Jenny in late 2003.

After Jenny received her Social Work degree in college, she began her professional career as a Home Based Counselor in Wooster, Ohio. A year later she accepted a position as a Case Manager for Gateway Woods in Leo, Indiana. Her position placed her front and center with domestic and international adoptions as well as foster care.

Jenny states, "I had no idea Zach was interested in me when he asked about Gateway Woods, or even over the next couple of years. There were moments during those years that I considered who I might marry someday, but Zach wasn't someone I was interested in because I saw him as goofy and immature. But, I also began to notice a serious side of him that was devoted to serving God and other people and I grew to respect that."

During that time, marriage for her was something for the future and not for now. Feeling an ideal time would be age twenty-five to thirty she wasn't anxious to make herself available anytime soon.

Jenny says, "Just to discourage potential suitors, I'd bring not-so-good food dishes to the youth group potlucks."

But then, in the fall of 2005, Jenny was attending the testimony of a convert in the Bluffton church. While praying, she heard God say, "You're going to marry Zach Bertsch."

Stunned, as she wasn't even thinking about marriage, she knew what she needed to do. From that point forward, she began praying for Zach.

Zach remembers the very beginning of his relationship with Jenny this way.

"One day in 2003, when I was 21, I had a strange thing happen to me while I was reading the 'Gate Post', the newsletter for Gateway Woods. I saw a picture of this beautiful young sister who had recently been hired as a Foster Care and Adoption Case Manager. As I looked at the picture of this smiling sister sitting at her work desk, I had the sudden conviction that this woman was to be my wife someday. The sister's name was Jenny Rufener from Smithville, Ohio. I had never met her before, but this feeling was very strong and unexplainable. I tried to shrug off these thoughts and just simply trust God for my future.

"Several months later, I decided to attend a singing with the Leo young group. During this singing, I couldn't help but notice the red-headed single sister that I had read about a few months earlier. After the singing, I was quick to introduce myself to her. We talked briefly about her new job at Gateway Woods and her love for adoption. She was a very nice sister and a Godly Christian woman.

"The following year, my dad, my brother Brad and I decided to buy a house in Fort Wayne and turn it into the 'Truckstop' for brothers from Bluffton to rent. Because of my involvement in the Truckstop, I also became more active in the Leo Young Group. I now saw Jenny frequently at 'Young Group' functions and was convinced she couldn't care less about me. She was always very nice, but I just didn't sense she had feelings for me. I was still very attracted to her as a Godly Christian woman, but I never felt pressed to ask for her hand in marriage.

"By May of 2006, I had been working full time for a year at Lincoln Financial and I had completed my first year of classes for my Master's in Business Administration. I was almost 24 years old and was still single. At this point in life, I was thinking about marriage, and I was thinking about Jenny more frequently."

On May 26, 2006, Memorial Day weekend, Zach drove several women, including Jenny, from Leo to Bluffton, Indiana. Enroute, he became lost several times. Jenny remembers, "I knew he was nervous having me in the car."

Zach recalls the trip. "The Leo Young Group met in Fort Wayne to carpool down to Bluffton to leave for a trip to Alabama. I drove a vehicle down to Bluffton that had two sisters in the back, one of them being Jenny. I was apparently a bit antsy and missed a few of my turns. One sister commented, 'You seem a bit nervous, Zach'.

"During the rest of the trip to Alabama, I tried my best to avoid Jenny and stay focused on the purpose of the trip, but it was difficult at times. At one point, I was especially nervous when I ended up sitting near Jenny during one of the meals and a conversation about the Song of Solomon came up."

Just prior to the Alabama trip, Zach had decided to submit a proposal for marriage to Jenny via Lynn Stieglitz, elder of the Leo church. Zach requested that it not be given to her until they returned from the trip to reduce awkward moments.

After the trip, on May 31st, Lynn told Jenny he had a proposal for her. He asked her to pray if she was ready for marriage.

A week later, on June 6th, Jenny told Lynn, "I believe I'm ready for marriage but there is a complication. I've been praying about a particular brother for six months and I'm not sure how I'll react if it's someone other than him."

Lynn hesitated, then said, "Well, the name is Zach Bertsch."

With a smile, Jenny said, "Okay! That's the man I've been praying for."

The next day, June 7th, Jenny told Lynn she had a peace to say 'yes' to Zach's proposal of marriage.

Today, Jenny says, "Praying for Zach for those six months helped me develop a love and relationship with him that was from God."

Lynn called Zach and told him Jenny had said, 'yes' to his proposal.

Zach said, "After I got off the phone with Lynn, I immediately called Jenny. She answered and we both struggled through some initial awkwardness before finally becoming comfortable we were actually talking to the person we would soon marry.

"I thought about meeting somewhere romantic for supper before church, but we eventually decided we would meet at McDonalds's, since we didn't have much time. During this meeting, we shared our stories and prayed together. We went to church separately and acted as if nothing was going on during the Young Group meeting. It was incredibly hard to contain my excitement. After church, we called our families and told them the news and could finally let the excitement out."

They were engaged on June 7, 2006 and married on September 24, 2006.

Of their relationship, Zach said, "Being married to Jenny meant that adoption and foster care were non-negotiable points."

Zach's mother Carmon said, "Jenny's love for orphans, adoption and foster care had a big impact on Zach."

Wedding Day – September 24, 2006
(Andrea Schafer – Credit)

Zach and Jenny's first year of marriage was busy as they balanced their relationship, vocational careers, Fort Wayne ministry opportunities and a pregnancy.

Jenny recalls, "During that first year in 2007, Zach had been working full time at Lincoln Financial Group and taking classes for his Master's Degree in Business. I was working full time at Gateway Woods. In late spring of 2007, Zach left Lincoln Financial Group to begin working at Gateway Woods as their Business Manager. Then things became even busier!"

Zion Michael was born on July 15, 2007. Zach remembers the day well.

"The day Zion was born, we were in the hospital over 20 hours before he was born. Jenny did a lot of walking the halls, and I was trying my best to encourage her.

"Then, at one point, when Jenny had pain, I started getting really dizzy and hot. I took off my outer shirt, and then the nurse saw me and told me to sit down immediately.

Zion Michael Bertsch – Born July 15, 2007

"The next thing I knew, I had several nurses around me, fanning me and putting a damp cloth on my forehead. I looked over at Jenny and she was about ready to clobber me! I eventually recuperated my nerve and didn't have any problems the rest of the delivery. We had narrowed the baby's name down to two names and it was after Zion was born that Jenny saw him and made the final decision. She looked at him and said, 'He's a Zion'!"

Jenny recalled, "After Zion was born, I continued working part time at Gateway Woods and Zach worked there full time. Looking back, I can see how Zach's time at Gateway Woods was very beneficial in teaching him the structure and operations of the non-profit world. He also developed an appreciation for the importance of long-term sustainability for non-profit organizations. That knowledge became a real asset later when working with Loving Shepherd Ministries and The Cancer Redemption Project (CRP)."

During that time working at Gateway Woods, Zach was also preparing for his upcoming CPA examinations. Jenny reflected, "Zach spent many nights studying with Zion strapped to his chest in a baby carrier so I could get some sleep.

"During that time Zach and I also volunteered for The International House in Fort Wayne. As a non-profit organization, they were devoted to refugees and other internationals seeking to acclimate to their new western home and culture. People were arriving in our area with little or no English, usually no relationships, many different religious beliefs and many questions. The International House became a vital link in helping them with their new life. It also gave us an opportunity for giving them a glimpse into a Christian's life."

Moriah Grace was born May 15, 2009. Zach recalls how that memorable day went.

"Moriah was born during a hard delivery as well. She was having a hard time coming out of the birth canal. I noticed the doctors and nurses start to panic and then I became really nervous too!

"With a new sense of urgency, I urged Jenny to push. The doctor tried one last maneuver before Jenny was going to need to have a dangerous, emergency C-section. It was then I desperately prayed to

God that he would answer my prayer and my baby girl could be born safely.

"All of a sudden, the doctor was able to twist Moriah and she came out. She was very blue but started breathing quickly. Tears ran down my face because I was so thankful for my answered prayer. This was the best and most important answered prayer of my life. I am so thankful to have my girl Moriah."

Moriah Grace Bertsch – Born May 15, 2009

At their home in Leo, Zach and Jenny poured themselves into their small family and loved and enjoyed Zion and Moriah. But, as with all marriages, with or without children, it wasn't always easy. Zach said, "We're both highly opinionated, so we had many 'strong discussions'!"

But one thing that wasn't up for discussion was their 'mutual' heart and interest for vulnerable children. In Zach's words, "Being married to Jenny meant that adoption and foster care were non-negotiable points."

Putting their mutual passion and faith into action, they became licensed as foster parents and did respite care for foster parents needing necessary breaks.

Then an opportunity arose for Zach. Becoming aware of an administrator's job opening at the Bluffton, Indiana Christian Care Retirement Community, he applied. With their home, church, work and extra-curricular activities all centered in Leo and Fort Wayne, this would be a big change if it transpired.

Jenny recalls the time. "After he applied for the job, we became aware that he wasn't the only applicant. That knowledge gave me peace because I wanted to stay in Leo. Having worked in a nursing home, I really wasn't sure the new job was a great fit for Zach. I thought that managing so many women would be difficult for him. I also believed the stress of working with residents and their families who were experiencing hard decisions and health problems would be tough.

"God worked in my heart as we waited to find out if he got the job. Just moments after I decided that I was okay with moving, Zach called me with the news that he was offered the position. I was able to give him my blessing to accept."

She continued, "Now, as I look at that period of time, it was evident that the job was God's way of moving us to Bluffton so we could be close to family as we went through the cancer battle. Another blessing was that Zach was prayed for by so many elderly Christians living at Christian Care. I am guessing their prayers were part of the reason Zach was able to do so many things in the last years of his life. They inspired him!"

Zach's family continued living in Leo while he commuted to Bluffton for several months until their home in Leo sold. Then they purposefully purchased a home large enough to be suitable for their dreams of having foster or adopted children in their family.

Their life was full and their dreams were bursting with vision and passion for their future.

Zach, regarding his marriage to Jenny, said, "The love that has grown between Jenny and me is absolutely amazing. It's truly a gift from our Father in Heaven. He knew our needs and sovereignly brought us together for His purposes. Our God is an awesome God who deserves all the glory and praise for drawing Jenny and me together and more importantly calling us to salvation and an unimaginable relationship with our Creator and Savior."

Family Photo - 2009

Family Photo – 2010 - (*Jenna M. Stoller – Credit*)

Family Photo – 2012 - (*Barb Roudebush – Credit*)

May 2012

Family Photo – April 14, 2013 - (*Pam Agler – Moments...by Pam* – Credit)

Zach's sister Cassie's wedding to Aaron Gerber – April 14, 2013
(*Pam Agler – Moments...by Pam* – Credit)

Chapter 9

TOWARD the end of 2009, Zach had been plagued with rectal issues which didn't seem to improve in spite of a variety of treatments.

Multiple visits to the doctor at the beginning of 2010 didn't add any value. In fact, Zach asked the doctor about a colonoscopy and the doctor said it was unnecessary. Finally, Zach ceased going to the doctor at that point and plunged headfirst into his new job at Christian Care Retirement Community.

Then, with the symptoms ongoing, a colonoscopy was scheduled for Saturday, June 12, 2010.

When Zach was in recovery, he asked the doctor, "Do I have cancer?"

The doctor hesitated and replied, "Yes. The mass was so large I couldn't complete the colonoscopy."

Zach felt 'numb'. Married less than 4 years, Zach was 27 years old, Zion was 2 and Moriah was 1 year old.

Two days later a CAT scan was performed. Zach and Jenny anxiously awaited word of the results. He described what happened next.

"The phone rang. I stared at it for a few seconds, knowing this was probably the most important call I would receive in my life. My office door was already shut, so I knew I could answer the phone in privacy. Finally, after four rings, I picked up the phone. It was indeed the call I was expecting.

"The doctor asked, 'Is this Zach Bertsch'.

"I replied, 'This is him'.

"He spoke softly, 'Zach, I'm sorry, but the CAT scan showed that there were some spots in both your liver and lungs. This doesn't mean that the spots are cancer. It just means we need to do a PET scan to find out what they are'.

"Tears immediately began to form in my eyes. I tried to hold back the flood of emotions, but was not succeeding. I knew what the spots meant. My life would never be the same and my life would be a lot shorter than I expected.

"I thanked the doctor and hung up the phone. I dropped my head into my hands and began to weep uncontrollably.

"Over the prior weekend, I had a colonoscopy and they had found a tumor. I had researched colon cancer on the internet all that evening. I knew that if the cancer had not yet spread, a simple surgery could be performed and 95% of people were cured. But if the cancer had spread to other organs, then only 4% of people live beyond 5 years. And even those 4% normally end up dying of the disease. The average life expectancy of someone with stage IV colon cancer was two and a half years. I knew I was in that category.

"I called Jenny and told her the news. We wept over the phone and then I said I was coming home. I left work and arrived home in five minutes. I fell into my wife's arms. She seemed to be stronger than I was.

"I stared at my two children with emptiness in my eyes. My little girl, Moriah, was only 1 year old and my little boy, Zion, was almost 3 years old. They were so young and innocent. Why did they have to lose a father? They couldn't understand what was going on but they knew that something was wrong.

"Jenny and I spent the rest of the day comforting each other as best we could. We called our immediate family members and told them the news, one by one. Each phone call felt like we were telling the same scary story over again. Each conversation ended with tears and sadness.

"At the end of the day, Jenny and I laid in bed exhausted. We prayed together and said our final comforting words before falling asleep."

On June 16, 2010, just two days after the CAT scan results, a PET scan was done to confirm the accuracy of the CAT scan.

The results confirmed the worst. It was stage IV colon cancer as it had spread to Zach's liver and lungs. There was no cure and life expectancy was 3 - 5 years.

Blood tests revealed Zach needed a blood transfusion due to his low hemoglobin count.

Ten days after the colonoscopy, Zach and Jenny had a meeting with Dr. Helft from the Indiana University Simon Center for Cancer. He said, "The cancer has moved from the colon to both the liver and lungs which means stage IV colon cancer. This type of cancer has no cure at this time, but we are thankful there are chemo treatments effective in shrinking the cancer and preventing it from spreading. Research has shown that people receiving treatment for stage IV colon cancer live for an average of two and one half years and one in eight live for five years. Your CAT scan results look like someone sprinkled a pepper shaker over your liver and lungs."

When Zach heard the doctor say, 'There's no cure', Zach said, "But, doc, there are miracles!"

The doctor replied, "Zach, I've seen a thousand of these and all of my patients died."

Zach felt 'shock and grief' when told the diagnosis. There were times of tears and heartbreak, but never did he ask, 'Why me'?

Zach's dad Mike said, "Zach got a grip and it helped all of us get a grip."

Over the course of his illness, neither Zach nor Jenny felt there would be a miracle of healing. They knew God could accomplish it, but didn't feel it was His will.

The doctor had said there were two regimens of chemotherapy which could be used, so the first was begun on June 29, 2010.

By the end of August, Zach's mind began to shift from earthly concerns to eternal visions...

Chapter 10

"I'M going to call Ed Schwartz for an appointment", Zach told Jenny.

As elder of the Bluffton Apostolic Christian church where Zach and Jenny were members, I wasn't surprised at receiving the call from them for an appointment. It wasn't uncommon for members of our church, at times of trauma in their lives, to set up a meeting.

The appointment was scheduled for Thursday, September 9, 2010 at 12:00 noon.

Upon arrival, Zach updated me on his health condition and cancer. He said, "The first rounds of chemotherapy are underway, the tumor in my colon has decreased in size, and the spots in my liver and lungs have decreased by 50%. The doctor has decided the time is right to remove the tumor, so surgery is scheduled for Friday, September 24th."

Then the meeting took an unexpected turn. Zach and Jenny weren't there to talk with me about discouragement, depression, fear, grief, the illness, healing, prayer or help.

Zach said, "We're here because of your organization, Loving Shepherd Ministries and what you do for orphans. With Jenny's and my love for orphans we want to do a project to redeem my cancer, but we don't have an organization to get a project done. We don't want to re-invent the wheel, so I was thinking if I can find the funds, LSM could do the project development, construction and ongoing work."

Then he said something that was profoundly Biblical and yet so magnificently unconventional that I was speechless.

"It seems when people get cancer, there's pain, surgeries, chemotherapies and sometimes death. I don't want my cancer to win. I want my cancer to pay the price for God's Kingdom work. I've been given a death sentence and I know I'm going to die sooner rather than later. I'm sad about that because I have a wife and two little kids I'm going to leave behind, but I don't want to waste my life. I want this cancer to do God's work."

Loving Shepherd Ministries, as an international non-profit organization, began in 2002 working with orphans; domestic and international adoptions; foster care in the U.S.; and orphan care on-the-ground in Haiti and Ethiopia.

Zach continued, "I want to use my cancer to bring glory to God and to be used to further His Kingdom. I want God to redeem my cancer. Does Loving Shepherd Ministries have a project you've wanted to do but didn't have the funds for?"

Surprised, I hesitated. "We'd like to build another Home of Hope in Haiti for twelve orphaned and vulnerable children. It would be for children who are orphans, restaveks or child-slaves who need a new lifetime family."

"Okay. That sounds good. Is that home in your budget?"

Still not quite understanding his vision, I said, "Yes."

"Well then, that won't work. This has to be something that wasn't going to get done unless my cancer made it happen. My cancer has to pay the price and be the reason this project materializes. Is there something you've dreamed about that you've wanted to do but couldn't, because you didn't have the funds?"

It was then I understood the glorious and selfless vision being laid out before me! I said, "We've always wanted to try a 'campus' setting of multiple homes in Haiti for orphans and child-slaves."

"Oh, how many homes were you thinking?"

"Four."

Zach responded, "I don't know if we could find the funds to build that many homes!"

In front of me was a young couple with faith, vision and passion. Of course, the diagnosis and prognosis had a very predictable outcome, but that didn't seem to dampen their enthusiasm. So, encouraged by their faith, I replied, "With your story and passion, I'm thinking God would bless your efforts."

Zach looked at Jenny and said, "I guess we could try and see how it goes."

September 9, 2010 marked the day a partnership began between Zach, Jenny and Loving Shepherd Ministries. His goal of speaking to individuals and groups to raise funds for orphans and vulnerable children in Haiti began quickly. Over the next two years Zach spoke to twenty-eight churches about his project known as 'The Cancer Redemption Project' or 'CRP'.

Almost immediately it was apparent the project was going to be blessed by God. The funding for CRP began to come in as Zach shared his passion for orphans and vulnerable children to anyone who would listen.

Chapter 11

THOUGH plagued with pain, surgeries and fatigue, Zach started sharing the vision of CRP to potential donors.

A week after having been diagnosed with stage IV colon cancer, Zach had begun his first regimen of chemotherapy. By September 1, 2010, the tumor had shrunk and the spots on his liver and lungs had diminished by 50%. So, on Zach and Jenny's fourth wedding anniversary, September 24, 2010, the surgeons performed a five hour surgery to remove the tumor.

A few days after the surgery, Zach experienced one of his most discouraging times which was soon offset by one of the most encouraging experiences in his life. He explained it this way...

"In September of 2010, I had my surgery to remove the main cancer tumor. There were several complications from the surgery and I ended up being in the hospital longer than expected. I was very sick and had severe pain during this time. One night, I was very discouraged and I prayed that God would give me an encouraging dream.

"That night I had the most crystal clear and beautiful dream that I have ever experienced in my life. I found myself alone in a deep, wide body of water, struggling to keep my head above the water. I looked all around and there was nothing but water in every direction.

"Exhausted, I gave up and began to sink. As I was sinking, my outstretched hand above me was the last thing to slip below the water surface. All of a sudden, a firm hand from above grabbed my outstretched hand and pulled me out of the water. I knew even before seeing Him that it was the hand of Jesus. Jesus pulled me into an air-filled rubber lifeboat. I was so thankful to be saved by Jesus.

"The odd thing was that I was not surprised at all, as I was expecting to be saved by Him. Jesus said nothing to me, but his smile and warm eyes told me everything. I knew that Jesus was taking me

Home to be with Him forever. I looked around me and there were several friends and family members in the lifeboat with me. I don't remember any specific person but everyone was smiling and thankful to be there.

"Jesus was standing at the front of the lifeboat and everyone else was sitting. The lifeboat hovered above the water and started racing forward. We soon saw a shore appearing in the distance. As we got closer we could see the excitement of those who saw the approaching lifeboat. There was a pier and several people ran to the end of the pier and dove off. The lifeboat quickly approached the people who dove into the water and Jesus pulled them in one by one. Somehow I knew each person, even though I didn't know them on Earth.

"The lifeboat continued on toward shore where people had run into the water and were now swimming toward the lifeboat. The lifeboat moved to each one and Jesus pulled them in with ease. Soon the lifeboat was full and everyone in sight had been safely pulled into the lifeboat.

"The lifeboat started rising and raced forward and upward into the clouds. It was a beautiful view to see the silhouette of the lifeboat in the clouds, with Jesus standing at front, leading us Home.

"Throughout the dream, there were times I experienced it as a third party observer. I was aware that it was a dream from God and an answer to my prayer. As I was still asleep, I was praising God for the dream. It was a beautiful assurance that God was with me and was going to take me to Heaven at the close of this trial.

"I awoke from the dream and immediately a smile came across my face as I thanked God for answered prayer."

Two and a half years after the dream, Zach said, "I have often looked back at this dream with confidence that God has been with me every step of the way. I have never doubted God's goodness. This dream has been a wonderful confirmation that Jesus will take care of me. I will rise again because He is my Savior, my lifeboat Captain."

In the days following the surgery, Zach had increasing pain as his abdomen began to swell. Two and a half liters of liquid were drained and it was determined that during the surgery his left ureter tube had been nicked and was leaking urine into his abdominal cavity. Additional surgery on the sixth of October attempted a repair.

During that stint in the hospital, Zach's scouting friend, Kellan Kershner decided to pay him a visit. Kellan remembers the visit well.

"I traveled to Indy to visit Zach at the hospital. Knowing his love for food, I stopped at Long's Bakery on 16th Street and picked up pumpkin flavored donuts. Zach loved donuts! I brought them up to his room. He was in a lot of pain and his taste was messed up. It was this visit when I first realized that my friend had a slim chance of remission and full health. They had removed nine inches of his colon and had nicked his ureter. It was a sad visit. Zach couldn't finish the donut, only eating a few bites."

Two days later Zach was released to go home, but unfortunately he continued to have swelling and pain. It became apparent there was an infection, so on October 21st another surgery was completed to deal with the abdominal infection and more leakage.

For the next months, things settled into a new norm for Zach, Jenny, Zion and Moriah. The new norm was saturated with constant pain and the powerful medications needed to manage the pain and still allow Zach to function. The new norm also included additional surgeries including one to reattach his ureter. Those were difficult weeks and months for Zach, Jenny and the family.

Jenny states, "It was hard on me when people would make comments on how good Zach looked. I felt that they didn't understand how hard his treatments were and how much pain he was in."

On June 21, 2011, one year after being diagnosed with cancer, Zach and Jenny drove to Indianapolis for a CAT scan.

The results showed Zach's cancer had grown since the last scan. As a result, the doctor recommended the second regimen of chemotherapy drugs should be started. It was a difficult thing to accept. There were only two chemo regimens which would possibly alleviate symptoms for Zach. The first one was no longer effective, so the second regimen seemed like their last hope.

Jenny's journal at the time recorded it this way – "Zach's battle with cancer continues and with it comes, dealing with pain, the side effects of the chemo treatments and the fatigue. The struggle to stay positive, keep hope and focus on the eternal also continues. Satan wants to distract our family from being shining lights for Christ and from seeking ways to further His Kingdom. We continue to move forward, held up on the prayers many have said on our behalf. We remain thankful for the glimpses God has given us of this cancer being used for good and our prayer is that others can continue to be touched by the work God is doing in our lives."

Two months later, another CAT scan revealed the cancer had not grown since starting the second round of chemotherapy. They felt blessed since this chemo worked only in about 30% of patients.

Chapter 12

THOUGH Zach persistently met with many individuals and groups during his illness, he still had to face the inevitable, ongoing issues of pain, treatments, doctor visits, surgeries and a predictable future.

On one side, he was focused on an eternal vision, while the other was fraught with the frailties of his humanness.

In October of 2010, four months after his diagnosis, he had written a few thoughts based on 2 Corinthians 5:7 – 'For we walk by faith, not by sight'.

My eyes see meaningless pain and suffering.
My faith sees a plan and purpose to bring souls to Christ.

My eyes see discouragement and despair.
My faith sees a reason to rejoice in the midst of trials.

My eyes see a pointless end in death.
My faith sees hope & promise for a much better future in Heaven.

Faith is the light in your heart...
When all your eyes see is the darkness ahead.

As I think about Zach's battle of the flesh and the Spirit, I'm reminded of Paul's words to the Corinthian church in 2 Corinthians chapter 4 – " [5] For we preach not ourselves, but Christ Jesus the Lord; and ourselves your servants for Jesus' sake. [6] For God, who commanded the light to shine out of darkness, hath shined in our hearts, to give the light of the knowledge of the glory of God in the face of Jesus Christ. [7] But we have this treasure in earthen vessels, that the excellency of the power may be of God, and not of us. [8] We are troubled on every side, yet not distressed; we are perplexed, but not in despair; [9] Persecuted, but not forsaken; cast down, but not destroyed; [10] Always bearing about in the body the dying of the Lord Jesus, that the life also of Jesus might be made manifest in our body.

11 For we which live are always delivered unto death for Jesus' sake, that the life also of Jesus might be made manifest in our mortal flesh. **12** So then death worketh in us, but life in you."

As funds began flowing in for the Cancer Redemption Project (CRP) at the end of 2010 and the beginning of 2011, a growing reality had to be faced. It was apparent the funds would be sufficient to build more than four Homes of Hope. So, Loving Shepherd Ministries began the search for a Haiti location to accommodate a campus.

On January 24, 2011, I met with the executive committee of a Haitian church denomination, with whom we had a long history of mutual trust, to discuss the project. As I shared Zach's illness and vision with them, the room grew quiet. Pastor Luders Erase, President of the 100,000 member MEBSH denomination, quietly said, "We find it almost impossible to comprehend what is happening with this young man named Zach and his young family. His vision is a beautiful and a wonderful project. Whoever heard of a young man wanting to do such a thing?"

We began exploring with them whether there was a current MEBSH location where they had a church and school that would accommodate a campus. They knew of nothing large enough to accomplish the vision. Then President Luders asked, "Would you consider building it where we don't have a church and school? Then you could build the homes for orphans, as well as create a new church and school?"

I assured them I would talk with the Bertsch's and evaluate the funding issues.

Upon returning to the U.S., I met with Zach and Jenny. They were exuberant about the idea of a church and school, and the incoming funds seemed to warrant the ever expanding vision.

The MEBSH executive committee began identifying potential regions and settled on the Cavaillon area, so Jan Gutwein, a missionary for LSM in Haiti, began a search for property.

After looking at ten different properties, he called me in February of 2011 from the eleventh location and said, "Ed, I'm standing on top of a small mountain outside of Cavaillon. The Spirit is telling me we've found our CRP location. I've got goosebumps and it's 90°! There's ten acres here that could work, but it's not going to be easy. It'll take a large bulldozer with a ripper blade to build a road to the top, as well as to prepare the home sites and the site for the church and school."

Negotiations began and in the spring of 2011, LSM owned a small mountain top in southwest Haiti.

The funds continued to come in for CRP as Zach untiringly shared his vision with others. Loving Shepherd Ministries now had the funds in hand to build six Homes of Hope for 72 vulnerable children, a church, school, fellowship center as well as a large pavilion where the children could play, study and the families could gather. We began working in earnest on the layout of the campus, the building designs, and developing an LSM construction team to do the construction.

As I think back to how God blessed Zach and Jenny, and their vision for the Cancer Redemption Project, I can think of many times where God did supernatural things to continually remind us that CRP was His vision and His project.

We now had a mountain and needed to build a road, as well as do all the excavation for the campus. We didn't have a bulldozer and we needed God to show up and take care of our next steps. We didn't know of any equipment available to us in Haiti to accomplish what we needed done. As a last resort, we could purchase a bulldozer in the U.S. and ship it to Haiti, but that would be costly.

As a next step, I purchased airline tickets to assist Jan Gutwein assess the construction problems and the campus layout. It was our slim hope that during my trip we possibly could find the equipment necessary to do the excavation work.

Enroute to Haiti on March 18, 2011, I was sitting at my gate in Fort Lauderdale, waiting to board my flight to Port au Prince. The airline desk attendant approached me and asked for my passport and economy ticket. He said, "I'll bring it back shortly." Confused and concerned, I waited. Ten minutes later he returned with my passport and a new first class ticket and told me I could board right away.

With outstretched legs and some minor degree of guilt, I soon had an orange juice in my hand along with some warmed cashews. Life was good and I thanked God for the unexpected blessing. But, anyone who serves the God of the universe knows He always has other plans than simply making us comfortable.

As I relaxed, I struck up a conversation with a white gentleman across the aisle. Assuming he was an American, I asked him why he was visiting Haiti. He said, "I live there."

"Oh, where?"

"I've lived in Port au Prince all my life, just as my parents and grand-parents did."

I continued the conversation, "What do you do?"

"I have a rental business."

Asking him what he rented, he said, "Construction equipment."

My attention piqued, I asked, "What kind of construction equipment?"

"Oh, the usual. Earthmoving equipment such as backhoes, trucks, excavators and bulldozers."

Astounded, I took the business card he held out to me. I told him we'd be in touch very soon.

Anyone who has spent time in a developing country knows the complexities of finding reliable equipment, efficient operators, finalizing contracts, and successfully completing projects. There was no doubt in my mind I'd just witnessed a miracle, delivered on God's golden platter! I wasn't seated in first class for my comfort. God talks about the fatherless in nearly 60 verses in His Word. He truly cares about vulnerable orphans.

The next day, Jan dialed the number of the rental equipment owner and asked about a bulldozer and availability. The rental business owner said, "I have a CAT D-7 bulldozer with ripper blade that would be perfect for what you want."

Having the perfect piece of equipment and a qualified operator available for the project was incredible. On August 7, 2011, the CAT D-7 bulldozer was delivered on site to CRP along with the Haitian operator. Two weeks later, the road was built and the pads for the six Homes of Hope, church, school and pavilion were all completed. There was even enough room on the property to level the ground for a large soccer field and playground. Construction of the foundations and concrete buildings were next.

The project required many tons of bagged cement for the footers, foundations, masonry, concrete walls and roofs. Though we had cement retail suppliers, being able to purchase directly from a wholesaler would significantly lower the construction costs.

I again purchased tickets to Haiti to assist in the next steps for the campus.

Sitting in the Fort Lauderdale gate area on November 16, 2011, enroute to Port au Prince, an airline desk attendant approached me and asked me for my passport. I had no anxiety at all, as I quickly handed it to her. I had no questions because now I knew what was happening. I remember quietly asking, "Lord, what are you up to now?"

She brought my passport back with a first class ticket and invited me to board. Upon boarding, I looked across the aisle and noticed a Haitian business man. He had no idea what was coming, nor did I.

I asked him, "Where do you live in Haiti?"

"I live in Port au Prince."

Cutting to the chase, I asked, "Oh, what do you do?"

He said, "I have a wholesale cement business. I import it and truck it by semi to worksites."

God is good all the time! I had a business card in my hand and we were off and running. I felt like I'd just witnessed another miracle delivered once again on God's golden platter.

Though LSM had a significant number of men already doing construction work for our various projects in southwest Haiti, the CRP campus construction was going to be on a whole new level. The number of buildings required and the complexity of construction for the school and church was going to be complicated. It would require more management, more experience and new techniques for our men to learn.

Randy Meyer from Chicago expressed interest in helping with the LSM construction. His many years of experience working with concrete, masonry and general construction became an answer to prayer as he poured himself and tons of concrete into the church and school project.

Randy has four passions. Construction projects; teaching about construction; sharing the Gospel; and discipling his construction crews. Bible devotions and prayers at the site were happening daily and those seeds bore fruit as construction workers were exposed and responded to the Gospel message over the next two years.

Chapter 13

CONSTRUCTION at the Cancer Redemption Project (CRP) continued. The ten acres on the mountain top was purchased in April of 2011, the site preparation was finished by September and construction began.

Work at the CRP Campus was accomplished with LSM Haitian crews managed by Maxon Clersaint, Christophe Sainvil, Jan Gutwein and Randy Meyer.

Jan Gutwein, Mike Bertsch, Maxon Clersaint and Zach

Jan Gutwein, Mike Bertsch, Christophe Sainvil and Zach

Randy Meyer

Mike, Zach, Brad and Ryan Bertsch breaking ground for the next home

By April of 2012 the progress was substantial. A half-mile road had been constructed to the campus and pads for the six Homes of Hope, church, school, soccer field and pavilion had been developed. Construction of two Homes were finished, a well had been drilled and LSM was ready to place the first two families in their new homes.

The children LSM places in the Homes of Hope have either lost both parents; lost one parent with the remaining parent unable to care for the child; both parents are living but unable to care for the child due to mental or physical illness or abandonment; has been rescued from a restavek child-slave situation; or the child is at immediate risk of becoming a restavek child-slave.

Wikipedia defines the Haitian restavek child-slave this way:

"A **restavek** (or **restavec**) is a child in Haiti who is sent by their parents to work for a host household as a domestic servant because the parents lack the resources required to support the child. The term comes from the French language *rester avec*, "to stay with". Parents unable to care for children may send them to live with wealthier (or less poor) families, often their own relatives or friends. Often the children are from rural areas, and relatives who host restaveks live in more urban settings. The expectation is that the children will be given food and housing (and sometimes an education) in exchange for doing housework. However, many restaveks live in poverty, may not receive proper education, and are at grave risk for physical, emotional, and sexual abuse.

"The restavek system is tolerated in Haitian culture, but not considered to be preferable. The practice meets formal international definitions of modern day slavery and child trafficking, and is believed to affect an estimated 300,000 Haitian children. The number of CDW (Child Domestic Workers) in Haiti, defined as 1) living away from parents' home; 2) not following normal progression in education; and 3) working more than other children, is more than 400,000. 25% of Haitian children age 5–17 live away from their biological parents." [2]

Restavek children generally work from dawn to dark carrying out the domestic chores for their 'caretaker' family. The children normally don't eat or sleep with the family, go to church or school and are denied health care. Often the family justifies what they're forcing upon the children, stating they would likely be living on the streets if they had not taken them into their home. The practice is considered bondage or slavery by the United Nations, as the children have no way to escape their work and aren't generally compensated. Often beaten and abused, the restavek practice is considered modern day slavery.

When the January 12, 2010 earthquake struck Haiti, the 7.0 magnitude quake plus the 5.9 and 5.5 magnitude aftershocks killed

2010 Earthquake *(Rick Schwartz – Photo Credit)*

an estimated 300,000 people. One million people were left homeless and countless children became orphans, many to become restaveks.

For placement in the Homes of Hope at CRP, LSM focused on children who were orphaned or became restaveks as a result of the earthquake.

The first step for LSM beginning a new Home of Hope is conducting a search for a Godly couple ready and able to be parents to twelve boys or twelve girls. The President of MEBSH, Alnève Emile and his executive committee assist by identifying locations for a home, then working with the local MEBSH pastor, deacons and LSM in finding a couple to fit the necessary parameters.

Some LSM couples are older and have already raised their biological family. But, they feel called to share their love, experience, the Gospel and life with a new family.

Other couples, considered infertile, prayed for biological children for years, to no avail. Being selected as parents of a Home of Hope and receiving twelve children is an answer to prayer for them.

New parents, as born again Christian believers, receive the full support of their church family as the next step is begun.

For the first homes at CRP, LSM staff in Haiti began talking to MEBSH pastors in southwest Haiti to find 'qualified' children. The search for CRP children, ages 3 - 9 years old, commenced and sadly, the numbers were staggering.

As the search continued, it was incredibly sad to know there were so many children who had suffered deep loss and grief and then were plunged into anonymity and obscurity. The encouraging thing was that at least 24 of them would soon have a new Haitian mom and dad, new siblings, a new home and a bright hope for their future.

LSM's orphan care model is unique in that it's modeled after God's definition of a family. The children in the Homes of Hope are provided a lifetime loving family devoted to God. They receive education, healthcare, trauma counseling, and resources for future vocational and university level training. They are given what's needed so they can become Godly country-changers helping to bring Jesus Christ into their Haitian culture.

LSM's model is rarely implemented in orphan care ministry around the world due to the associated costs and the comprehensive continuum of care required to do it well. Sadly, institutionalized care and orphanages have become the norm with children missing out on God's original design of the 'family model'.

There are an estimated 30,000 children living in 760 Haitian orphanages, according to the J.K. Rowling charity LUMOS. Nearly all of these institutionalized children age-out of those facilities at 18 years old. They generally enter Haitian life, ill equipped with little skills or resources, to begin their new lives.

Zach stated, "Jenny and I were drawn to LSM's model because we love the concept of adoption. LSM treats orphans in a way God designed, by placing them into lifetime families with a Godly mom and dad."

On April 16, 2012, nearly two years after Zach was diagnosed with stage IV colon cancer and given three to five years to live, he, Jenny and some of their extended family arrived in Haiti to see the Cancer Redemption Project first-hand. The larger purpose of their arrival in Haiti was to interview nearly 40 children in their mission to fill the first two CRP Homes of Hope with 24 kids.

When it became apparent funding would permit the construction of six Homes of Hope, Zach and Jenny wanted to give each family a unique and meaningful Biblical name.

Zach shared, "The first home is named 'Ezekiel Home of Hope', because my nickname was 'Ezekiel' when I was little and many memories surround that name.

"The second home is named 'Abba', because that refers to one of Jenny's favorite verses in Romans about adoption, where we call God, 'Abba', or Father.

"The third and fourth homes are 'Mount Zion' and 'Mount Moriah', named after the Biblical mountains our children are named after.

"The fifth and sixth homes are called 'Daniel' and 'Esther', because those are some of Zion's and Moriah's favorite Bible characters and they represent people of great courage for following God."

Courtney Pfister, a close cousin to the Bertsch family, remembers the Home of Hope 'naming' process.

"Zach and Jenny had named the first two homes and were now flying to Haiti to name, dedicate and fill the third and fourth homes. I had heard they were going to name them Zion and Moriah, so I texted them and said, 'I'm disappointed you didn't name a home after me'! So, when Zach and his family got back from Haiti, they sent me a video. It showed an outhouse on the CRP property. In the video, the outhouse door opened and Zach's brother Ryan stepped out. He pointed to a sign on the door which read 'Courtney's Corner'. The Bertsch boys were always good for a laugh."

The task before Zach and Jenny during the April, 2012 trip was daunting, as the interviews of the 40 children began. One by one the children were brought into the room and their histories were explored and documented. The stories of tragedy, the earthquake, loss of parents, injury, fear, abuse and hopelessness were crushing and dark.

Looking into the eyes of each child, it was obvious they were carrying deep and personal pain. There were tears from some of the children as they sought to comprehend what was taking place. There were tears from the onlookers as well, as again and again, they were plunged into the depths of sadness for the children.

But, at the end of the interviews, tears and prayers, Zach and Jenny had selected the 12 boys and 12 girls for the Ezekiel and Abba Homes of Hope. The rest of the children departed to go back to their hopeless life. Except now, their history and data was in an LSM database to be considered for one of the next four homes.

Two days later, 24 boys and girls excitedly walked into their new homes and met their new mom and dad. Zach and Jenny participated in a dedication ceremony committing the homes and two families to a life of fulfilling God's plan of redemption.

Zach talked often about 'Home'. As he watched Haitian children become a part of their new 'home', it solidified his personal and eternal perspective about his own life. Having the opportunity to see the reality of his vision and being able to witness faith becoming sight, stirred him greatly. Knowing he would soon make the journey 'Home' became an ongoing and positive focus.

To emphasize the concept, *Psalm 100*, a Gospel quartet (Zach's brother Ryan and three friends) recorded a CD titled 'Home', filled with songs about Heaven. It was a huge blessing to many and spoke Zach's heart which prompted his innermost thoughts.

"I was diagnosed with stage IV cancer in 2010. Unless God provides an absolute miracle, I will be going Home soon. As I think of Home my heart is stirred with passion for my true Home, as well as a burden for the many lost souls who need Jesus.

"Early on in my battle with cancer, I realized there seemed to be two choices when faced with suffering. We can choose to let the suffering make us better, or allow it to make us bitter. If we allow the suffering to make us better we can redeem the trials for God's glory.

"We can face our trials with Godly courage, as courage isn't the absence of fear, but rather the realization that 'someone' is more important than fear, and that 'someone' is Jesus Christ, the one worthy of all of our praise.

"Christ is able to use my life, my cancer, even my death for His glory. I actually get excited at times about the possibilities of how the Lord can use my cancer to accomplish His purposes. My greatest desire is that just one more soul will be in Heaven because of my cancer. I believe we were made to give ourselves to this great eternal cause of sharing the Gospel of Christ. This truth in the total perspective carries me through my deepest suffering and darkest nights."

Some of Zach and Jenny's family members interviewing
children for Ezekiel and Abba Homes of Hope in April, 2012

Zach's dad Mike

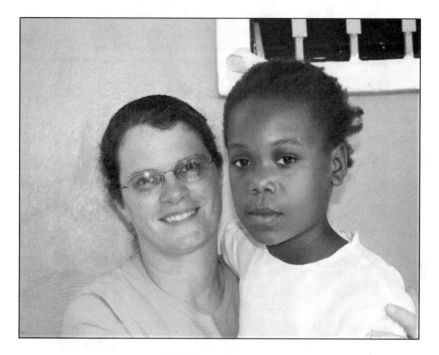

Zach's mom Carmon

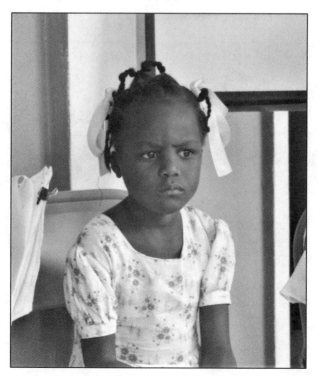

Jenny's mom Janice

Children waiting for their interview opportunity

Zach's brother Ryan with twin orphans being interviewed

Zach and Jenny during an interview

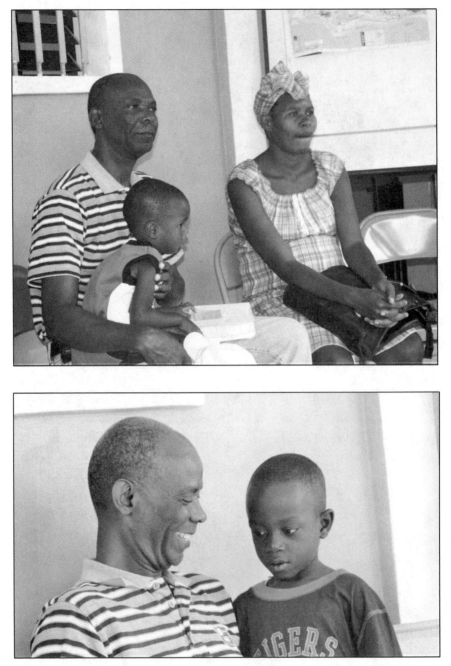

Loving Shepherd Ministries Director of Home of Hope Operations, Pastor Wilfrid Remonvil – Responsible for finding the children who are placed in LSM's homes, as well as their ongoing care.

Another boy for the Ezekiel CRP Home of Hope

20 of the 24 boys and girls on the way to their new
Ezekiel and Abba Home of Hope families

Exploring their new Abba Home of Hope at the
Cancer Redemption Campus in April of 2012

Gade ki jan Papa a renmen nou
non! Li sitelman renmen
nou li rele nou pitit li
1 Jan 3: 1
Behold what manner of love the Father hath
upon us, that we should be
called children of God.

Zach sharing thoughts with the Abba and Ezekiel children

Chapter 14

BETWEEN April and December of 2012, Zach was determined to communicate the message of The Cancer Redemption Project to as many people as possible. During that time, he shared the CRP opportunity to ten different churches. Though pain and fatigue continued to drag him down, his passion drove him on.

Kellan Kershner, Zach's scouting friend, visited him and later said, "Zach was in a lot of pain or discomfort. The thing that struck me was the struggle Zach had in providing structure for the kids, spending time with his family, and his pain and health needs. It was a challenge I never contemplated families needing to manage."

Though Jenny was an integral part of Zach's vision for The Cancer Redemption Project, she tried to keep the family 'as normal as possible', as Zach's symptoms and cancer worsened.

She remembers the balancing act. "The hardest part of the journey for me was that Zach would pour himself into a presentation and get intense pain. He gave all he had to CRP and sometimes there was little left for me and the kids."

That simple statement carries with it the reality of Zach's passion and determination; Jenny's willingness to let Zach fulfill his last days with excellence; and their undying love for one another.

Viewing first-hand the rapid development of the CRP campus and being able to personally place the first 24 children in the Ezekiel and Abba Homes of Hope was a powerful boost to Zach and Jenny. But, the cancer was continuing to take its inevitable toll.

It seemed the never-ending battle of the flesh against the Spirit was a perpetual struggle leading to a predictable end.

In December of 2012, Zach, Jenny and some of their extended family made another trip to Haiti. The third and fourth Homes of Hope were finished and parents were waiting for their new children.

Jenny recalls the trip in her journal.

"We've just returned from our second trip to Haiti and the opening of Mount Zion Home of Hope for boys and the Mount Moriah Home of Hope for girls. Ten orphaned boys and seven girls now have parents and siblings. There is space for two more boys and five more girls to move into the homes in the next few months.

"Our trip included playing with the 24 children we placed in April as well as wonderful fellowship with their parents and other LSM staff. As I looked over the campus, I was amazed by how much has been done in such a short period of time. What was an empty hill two years ago is now a thriving home for 41 children and their new parents.

"The construction, gardens and landscaping work has provided jobs for over 50 Haitian people. Gardens are growing to provide food for the campus and fruit trees are abundant to provide food in the future. Many dump truck loads of stone have been brought to the church and school location and construction is scheduled to start in early 2013. Land has been leveled for the fifth and sixth Homes of Hope, which we've named Daniel and Esther. We're hopeful the construction for those two homes can start before the end of 2013.

"One of my favorite Bible verses is 1 Peter 1:17 – 'That the trial of your faith, being much more precious than of gold that perisheth, though it be tried with fire, might be found unto praise and honor and glory at the appearing of Jesus Christ'.

"We feel like our faith has been tried over these past two and a half years more than any other time in our lives. Many days we wonder how we can press on, or if God can really use us in our weak human bodies. I often get frustrated at my human limitations and I know Zach feels the same way. While we hate the suffering and struggles, we are so thankful that God is giving us a wonderful glimpse of how He is using the trials we are facing to bring Praise, Honor and Glory to His Name."

While on the December, 2012 trip to Haiti to fill the Zion and Moriah Homes of Hope, Zach shared some of his heart.

Leaning on a rustic, blue and white, wooden sailboat used by local fishermen, with the turquoise waters of the Caribbean in the background, he said: "I've heard it said, that life isn't a pleasure cruise gliding on  the sea of life. It's a battleship stationed on the very gates of hell.

"Life isn't easy. We're not meant to live easy lives. We are meant to fight for a cause, live for our King, to carry out His Great Commission. That commission ought to take sacrifice, devotion and commitment. Doing things that we don't always want to do, that aren't easy, and aren't comfortable.

"But the rewards will be great and all of eternity will be different and better. There will be more people there, praising our Lord, if we live for Him right here, right now, doing the hard things that win souls and save lives for all eternity."

On that same trip, we passed a Haitian cemetery where colorful concrete burial crypts are used. Many have ornate concrete crosses on top. Leaning back against one of the burial vaults with the cross towering above him, Zach said, "I'm standing in a cemetery, because it reminds me of how short life is. Life is a vapor. It passes away. It's like a blade of grass that is cut. It's a flower that wilts and fades away.

"But there are things that last for eternity – our souls. Our bodies will be resurrected and our souls will last for eternity. But the things that we spend our time on, many of them will be wasted. But the things that benefit the Kingdom of God will last forever.

"We should live for the 'line' and not the 'dot'. Eternity is like a line that will go on forever and ever. We'll look back at this little dot that is our life, and wish we had done so many things different. We would wish we had allocated our time, our resources, our money, our treasures and possessions in building the Kingdom. Please join me in living for the line and not the dot. Our bodies are going to end up underneath a tombstone, buried, and there will only be certain things that last for eternity. Spend your time and your resources on those things that last forever."

As if the balancing act between his cancer, the Cancer Redemption Project, speaking engagements and devoting time to his family wasn't enough, Zach with his brothers pursued another vision. Together, they wrote a Daily Devotional titled, *'Prepare to Die and Then Live'*.

There were 365 thought provoking devotions in the book filling twelve different categories.

- Realizing God's love and loving him in return
- Dying to self
- Loving the Word and prayer
- Experiencing God's power and grace
- Loving righteousness and hating sin

- Living in true humility
- Living in joy and contentment
- Loving others and becoming a fisher of men
- Realizing it's all about Jesus
- Living for the Kingdom and our true Home
- Embracing suffering and death
- Anticipating resurrection and eternity

Sometimes, someone will ask the thought provoking and philosophical question, "What would you do if you were given three days or three months or three years to live?"

We would likely have a few ideas about our need to mend a relationship or two, spend more time in the Word and prayer, or checking something off our bucket list.

When Taunia Henry of Gridley, Illinois heard Zach's story of redeeming his cancer and the Cancer Redemption Project, she felt inspired to write a song. That song was very meaningful to Zach and many others.

Six Months to Live
Words and Music by Taunia Henry

What would you do if you knew
That you had six months to live?
What would you say, where would you go, what would you give
As you fought the fight and lived the dream?
Ain't it funny how life isn't what it seems?

What would you do if you knew
That you had six months to live?
Would you leave your cares behind and follow Him?
Would you preach His Word across the sea?
Would you help the hungry child so in need?

What would you do if you knew

That you had six months to live
Before you stood before the mighty judgment throne
To give account for what you've done
With your life and with God's own begotten Son?

For we all as a vapor pass away,
And not one of us is promised to live another day!
So redeem the time and strive to give
Like a child of God who has six months to live!

No one asked Zach, to my knowledge, that philosophical question, after he was diagnosed with stage IV colon cancer and given three to five years to live. But, those who knew him simply got out of his way and watched as he passionately lived out the rest of his life in his answer to that question.

People had observations as they watched Zach *'Prepare to Die...'*

"Once Zach got something in his head, there was no stopping him."

"He reminded me of a steer in a 'calf-roping' contest at a rodeo. Once the gate opened, the steer was off and running and all you could see were tail-lights."

"When he was growing up, we saw his persistent, competitive, tenacious and get-er-dun nature. That served him well all the way to the end."

"He was an ornery kid growing up who seemed to attract trouble, but when he came to Christ, that all changed. All his energy was now spent in serving God."

"When I think about Zach's life, I think about a quote from Hunter S. Thompson – 'Life should not be a journey to the grave with the intention of arriving safely in a pretty and well preserved body, but rather to skid in broadside in a cloud of smoke, thoroughly used up, totally worn out, and loudly proclaiming - Wow! What a Ride!'" [3]

The Daily Devotional is an inspiration to many, not only in its content, but with the concept that all the books' proceeds went to furthering CRP. It was easy to be inspired by Zach's outlook for death and eternal life. The devotional he and his brothers wrote, solidified that. Zach's prologue for the Devotional summed up his life prior to cancer and certainly after.

"I have thought a lot more about death lately. This is understandable since I've been diagnosed with stage IV cancer. I have been surprised that it has been good to think about death. Our death will be the biggest moment in our lives. It will be our grand entrance into God's presence in Heaven. It has been good for me to prepare for the moment everything will change. I want to be ready to die and ready to live.

"As I examine my life in light of eternity I realize that we aren't made to live like most people. We were made to fight a spiritual battle. We were made to give ourselves to a cause that is eternal. We are to give our lives to advance a Kingdom. And to fight for our King. We are to live with a passion and a fire in our eyes. Let's be totally committed and know that it will cost us. We were made for this. We were made to set aside our little temporal causes and give ourselves to this one great battle. We pray that this devotional can be a tool for Christians in the battle for the souls of men.

"Another thing that I realize in thinking about death, is how our view of death and eternity drives how we live our lives. There are many things that we would not bother to do, if we only lived here on Earth but that we had better care about very much if we are going to live forever. We need to start living for Heaven in sending treasures ahead - Matthew 6:33. We need to make sure that everyone knows about Heaven and Jesus. May these daily thoughts remind us of our high calling.

"If Heaven is so great why don't we long to be there? Because we have the wrong impression of it. Satan has used false impressions of Heaven to steal the joy of believers, instill fear in those who are dying, and to reduce the desire for unbelievers to want to be there. Maybe the reason that we can't quite feel truly at home anywhere on this Earth is because Heaven is our true home. For eternity we will be with Jesus the Person that we were made for, living in Heaven, the place that we were made for. We pray that these devotions help us to realize and then long for our eternal Home with Jesus.

"Finally my prayer for everyone reading this daily devotional is that we would all take steps to ensure that we don't waste our life. We've only been given one life... it may be a few decades, or it may be a century but it's still very, very short. It's just as easy to waste a long life as it is to waste a short life. When I mean waste our life, I mean living for things with no eternal benefit. What will we have to show for our life in the end, after the earthly cares and concerns disappear?

"These daily devotions are thoughts, scripture, and quotes from a group of brothers that love each other and love our brothers and sisters in Christ. We have benefited the most by writing these devotionals and thinking about them. Our prayer is that many more would benefit from serious daily reflection on the Word of God and the power that it has to change lives. Thank you to all that have supported us in prayer and in love. In His Grip - Zach Bertsch"

Prior to being diagnosed with cancer, Zach had already been thinking about what he wanted to achieve in life, so he developed a 'bucket list' of fifty things he'd like to accomplish before he died. Among the fifty things, ten of them were powerfully fulfilled by The Cancer Redemption Project.

1. Adopt a child or children from another country.

7. Use financial resources for spreading the Gospel.

19. Always serve Christ and have a 'Kingdom Mindset'.

27. Start up a business or ministry on the side at home with Jenny.

36. Show compassion to orphans.

38. Show compassion to strangers.

43. Go on another work team to Haiti.

48. Be known as an encourager.

49. Have a 'good name' to pass down to my children.

50. Be faithful to Christ 'til death'.

As 2012 relentlessly flowed into 2013, life continued to roll forward as Zion and Moriah grew older, the CRP campus was being built and Haitian children were given new life and hope.

But, Zach's earthly life was winding down.

Chapter 15

NOT only was Zach passionately forging ahead with the CRP campus, he likewise was busy encouraging people to not 'waste' their life.

He knew it was vital for him to develop and achieve Biblically based core values and principles in his own life prior to giving advice to others. Early in his Christian life, he developed his "Life Purpose" and was committed to following that purpose until his death.

"I am alive to serve God with everything I've been given. Therefore, His laws and the "Fruits of the Spirit" are the guiding principles of my life. My goals, whether family or career related, should all fall in line with my overall reason that God has me on this earth. If this is true, then the actions and direction of my life should match my overall goal to maintain a 'Kingdom Mindset' and share the love of Christ with everyone around me."

Likewise, he felt a specific need to encourage men to become *'Mighty Men of Christian Valor'*. He developed the topic in February of 2013 and shared it with many men.

Top 10 Mighty Man of Christian Valor Traits
Note: Reference to 'brothers' is non-biological

1. He is a leader of the home, setting the standard of purity and holiness. He is proactive instead of reactive, by confronting evil, pursuing justice, and loving mercy with Godly wisdom and balance.
2. He loves prayer and has a daily relationship with God. He loves communicating with his Father in Heaven.
3. He is always right with Christ because of repentance, asking for forgiveness, and confession. He is often the first to genuinely ask for forgiveness (even if he feels that he is right) – especially with his wife and brothers. He confesses his faults easily in specific

detail to those who need to know. He realizes that he isn't perfect and, therefore, he doesn't come across as self-righteous.

4. He cuddles with his wife often in a non-sexual way, always passionately dedicated to fulfilling her emotional needs as a top priority. (Loving her according to knowledge – 1 Peter 3:7-9)

5. He spends time with his young children purposefully teaching them spiritual and life lessons. He spends time with his teenage children doing what they want to do in order to meet them where they are at and seeking life lesson teaching opportunities.

6. He is loyal to his church and his brothers. He pursues a comradery with his brothers fighting side by side with them – seeking accountability and providing it for other brothers.

7. He views the Great Commission as a personal mission from the King of Kings. He pursues the saving of souls, especially through the avenue of the fatherless, widow, and foreigner.

8. He is zealous and passionate for the Lord and for his family. He is known for his spiritual conversations and his interest in scripture and love for the Lord. (Phil. 3:7,8)

9. He pursues his work as unto the Lord and thinks often about the greater purpose in witnessing at work and using his financial gain for the Kingdom. (Col. 3:1,2,23)

10. He does not fear death and doesn't play life safe. Instead, he is willing to risk it all for Christ.

Top 10 Signs of a Lack of Christian Valor
(Being a Lukewarm, Selfish Christian)

1. He lacks leadership in the home, allowing sinful television and internet usage to waste his time. He is only reactive, often avoiding the confrontation of evil by not addressing the issues.

2. He doesn't pray often and doesn't view God as a close Father. He doesn't enjoy communion and a closeness with God.

3. He is sometimes not right with Christ because he is slow to repent, ask for forgiveness, and confess his sins. He is rarely the first to genuinely ask for forgiveness. He is stubborn and stuck in his ways, especially with his wife and brothers. He rarely confesses faults in specific detail. He sticks to generalities and takes the moral high ground with his words by making others think that he is super spiritual.

4. He does not cuddle with his wife often or say I love you in a non-sexual way. He only does these things when he is fulfilled sexually.

5. He spends little time with his young children in purposeful teaching. He spends little time with his teenage children in doing what they want to do and purposefully maintaining a positive relationship with them.

6. He is not loyal to his church and doesn't pursue a bond of brotherhood. He doesn't make himself available to serve other brothers and doesn't pursue brotherhood opportunities.

7. He is not directly engaged in the Great Commission. He just hopes that it may happen as part of his divided Christian life. He doesn't personally stand up for the weak, and doesn't have time for the orphan, widow, or foreigner.

8. He is really not zealous or passionate for the Lord. He rarely brings up spiritual issues unless there is an agenda he wants to fulfill. He is not known or defined by his love for the Lord.

9. He pursues work as an ego-fulfilling part of life that is separate from his spiritual life.

10. He fears death and plays life safe. He is pursuing the American Dream instead of Christ.

Chapter 16

SPRING of 2013 began to gently nudge the winter months into the background. In Indiana, new life was being breathed into the trees, grass and flowers. In Haiti, new life was just as evident as we watched the lives of forty-eight former orphans in their new homes at CRP begin to blossom and bloom. Most were experiencing Jesus Christ, safety, stability, family, love and hope for the first time.

But in spite of being surrounded by new life, Zach's pain continued to worsen. His energy was rapidly declining. The chemotherapy, though helping for a time, was now finished. Little more could be done other than to rest, manage pain levels with drugs, and try desperately to enjoy life with his family and friends.

Jenny recalls the time. "On March 7, 2013, Zach had an outpatient surgery so the doctors could insert a pain pump. The goal was for better pain management with fewer oral medications that made it hard for him to think. The surgery was successful but he had to be hospitalized for three days to address his pain and an infection. On March 29th, Zach had his final visit at Indiana University Health. Dr. Helft told us that Zach's body was declining and any further treatment wouldn't be helpful. Zach was admitted to Hospice on April 1st."

Jenny's Journal entry – April, 2013

"I remember praying with my bridesmaids before walking down the aisle on the day of our wedding that our wedding and marriage would glorify God. I could say a lot about our six years of marriage. There have been so many good times and there have been challenging times when we had to deal with each other's weaknesses. Through it all God has been faithful.

"As I face the reality that my husband's life is coming to an end my heart breaks. I have come to depend on Zach for so much. Even when he is in pain he provides me with so much emotional support.

At the end of a long day I can still count on him to listen to me talk and hold my hand. I dread facing life without him.

"As I pray now, I often ask God to fill the places in my life that will be left empty. I know in my mind that Jesus can and will provide for my needs, but at times I struggle to feel it in my heart. I pray that Jesus will be more real to me than He has ever been. I pray that He will give me courage to step forward in faith, knowing that my Great God can provide everything I need to bring Him Glory."

Jenny's Journal entry – May 5, 2013

"Dear Lord, Please help me to learn and grow so I can be used by You. I'm scared, Father. Every day I watch Zach get weaker. He has lost so much weight and sleeps more. He is hungry, but gets sick when he eats. He has open wounds that are getting worse, Lord. He longs to go Home, Father, and I struggle to know how to let him go. I don't know how I will survive without the man you appointed to be my earthly protector, companion and best friend.

"Part of my fear comes in thinking about the future. If it's your plan to take my husband home at a young age, is it possible that You will also ask for one or both of my children? How do I keep myself from being paralyzed by fear? How do I stay focused on the fact that Zach, Zion, and Moriah are all Yours. Am I willing to give them completely to You to be used for Your glory? Can I rest in faith that You are my God? That You want the best for me. That You want to use the life You have given me to bring You glory.

"You are worthy of every tear that I cry. You are worthy of every emotional and physical pain I suffer. You alone deserve my praise. You alone can fill all the broken places of my heart. You can use this weak woman with all my failures for purposes greater than myself. Help me to be willing to give everything to You. In Jesus Name, Amen."

On May 16, 2013, just twenty-one days before he passed away, Zach sent a devotion to family and friends. He said, 'I can certainly relate to this poem... and I'm sure many of you can too'.

A Prayer of Weariness – by Randy Alcorn [4]

I AM WEARY, Lord... bone tired.
Weary to the point of tears, and past them.
Your Word says you never grow weary
But I know you understand weariness
Because once you drug a heavy cross
up a long lonely hill.
Many times you had nowhere to lay your head
And people who needed you pressed upon you
by day and by night.
My reservoir is depleted, almost dry.
For longer than I can remember I've been
dredging from its sludgy underside
Giving myself and my loved one the leftovers
of a life occupied with endless tasks.
The elastic of my life is so stretched out of shape
that it doesn't snap back anymore.
Just once I'd like to say "It Is Finished," like you did.
But you said it just before you died.
I guess my job won't be over till my life is
and that's OK Lord, if you'll just give me strength to live it.
Deliver me from this limbo of half-life;
Not just surviving, but thriving.
You who know all, You who know me
Far better than I know myself-
Deposit to my account that as I spend myself
There may be always more to draw from.
Give me strength
To rest without guilt...

To run without frenzy...
To soar like an eagle
Over the broad breathless canyons of the life
You still have for me both here and beyond.

I visited Zach that same afternoon on the sixteenth of May. He spoke about things near and dear to his heart. On his mind were his family in the U.S. and his 'new' family in Haiti. He wanted to record a video message for the families and children at CRP. As he laid on his bed, his head propped up on a pillow with Jenny by his side, he gave his last words to his precious Haitian families. His voice was weak and tears streaked his face as he quietly said...

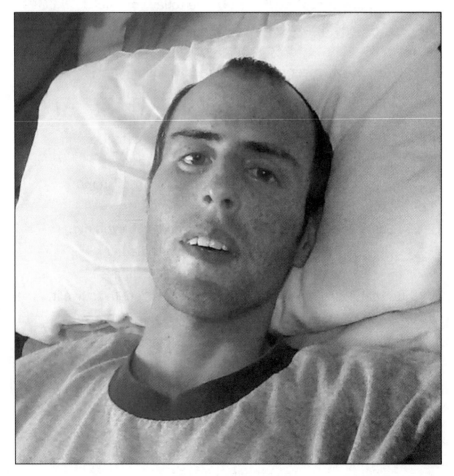

"Well, it's been a long journey. Now here we are in the middle of May and the Lord still has me alive for a purpose. I'm praying that I can find joy in each day. Sometimes I have mountains and valleys, but one of the things that keeps me going is my eyes fixed on Heaven. I'm so excited to see Jesus and get to Heaven. If you know baseball, I feel like I'm rounding third base and I'm heading home.

"I want to say that the people and children in Haiti are my biggest cheerleaders. I think of you guys often in how we got to be a part of your lives. It never would have happened if I hadn't gotten cancer. So all of this, even this ending, ties back to your lives and the blessings we've had in having crossed paths and having me be able to share Christ with you and you encouraging me in my Christian faith. It's been a beautiful thing.

"To the very end I'll be thankful for that. In fact there's going to be a picture of some Homes of Hope on my tombstone. So, that just shows you how special it is to me... and a quote that says, 'If by my death or by my cancer, God has been given more glory, or if more souls have come to Christ, then it's been worth it all.' That gives me a lot of joy in these end times. Thank you for what you're doing. Keep pressing on in the Lord, draw close to Him. We'll never regret it."

The following day, on May 17th, Jenny wrote the following to their family and friends.

"Zach remains peaceful. He is so ready to go 'Home', but continues to rest in the fact that if he is still on this earth God has things for him to do. God blessed him with conversations with several people in the last week that were good reminders of the fact that God is still using him.

"His body is sensitive to touch and he spends most of his time in bed. Zach normally sleeps from midnight to around two o'clock each afternoon. He eats very little now, because eating often makes him feel sick. The doctors have told him only to eat if he wants to, because his body does not absorb food very well anymore. It's hard to see him lose weight, but I remind myself that soon he will have a new healthy body in Heaven. Zach has pain, but the pain medications are making it bearable.

"For those who know Zach well, you know he likes to talk. Over the past few weeks he has been talking less. He enjoys company, but prefers to listen to other people talking around him rather than participating in the conversation. When he does talk, Jesus and Heaven are often his topic of conversation. His voice is softer now, making it harder for people to understand him on the phone.

"I have been trying to make life as normal as possible for the kids. Zion has been going to school and both kids have spent time with friends. Zion started playing T-Ball on a team with some of his friends last night. We went to the zoo with Zion's pre-school class on Wednesday and played at the park with friends yesterday. Moriah had a great fourth birthday celebration with family Saturday night.

"I am taking one day at a time. It's hard knowing that at any moment I could find Zach not breathing and I often wonder how I will respond. I am thankful that we have been able to talk about his death and our family's future a lot over the past weeks and months.

"Zach has had a lot of help from family and friends to create special books and DVD's for the kids. This has been a huge blessing to me since I was rather overwhelmed by the projects I wanted him to do for them. Each day, one of my goals is to rest in faith instead of allowing fear to overwhelm me.

"This song is in my thoughts today:

Turn Your Eyes Upon Jesus – Helen H. Lemmel (1922) [5]

O soul are you weary and troubled?
No light in the darkness you see?
There's light for a look at the Savior
And life more abundant and free

Turn your eyes upon Jesus
Look full in His wonderful face
And the things of earth will grow strangely dim
In the light of His glory and grace

Through death into life everlasting
He passed, and we follow Him there
Over us sin no more hath dominion
For more than conquerors we are

And turn your eyes upon Jesus
Look full in His wonderful face
And the things of earth will grow strangely dim
In the light of His glory and grace

His word shall not fail you, He promised
Believe Him and all will be well
Then go to a world that is dying
His perfect salvation to tell

And turn your eyes upon Jesus
Look full in His wonderful face
And the things of earth will grow strangely dim
In the light of His glory and grace

Zach's younger sister Cassie has two vivid memories of Zach's last days on earth.

"The thing that meant the most to Zach was 'Living like Christ and not just talking about Him'. While he was heading to his last day, a lot of people assumed that he had some fears about death. Maybe he did. I remember his biggest fear was that Jenny would raise their kids by herself and be alone. He was adamant about having a 'lone' gravestone and made it very clear he wanted her to remarry. She meant the world to him and what an example that was!"

The other memory Cassie has is more personal. "I'll never forget the last words Zach ever said to me. In the last week of his life, he didn't talk much, but Aaron and I still went to visit him. In fact, he was mostly unconscious in that final time. During our last visit with him, he was sleeping on the couch. Something made him wake up and sit up. He was stumbling to his bedroom when he noticed me in a glimpse of clarity. 'Love you', he whispered. I smiled. Even half-conscious, his heart was there. Those words in that moment sum up my brother Zach Bertsch."

Chapter 17

JENNY'S Journal entry – June 6, 2013 (the day Zach passed away)

"I thank You, Father, for the last day I spent with Zach. It was hard to wake up at 3:30 in the morning and see him uncomfortable and not be able to understand him. Please help me to let go of the burden of the things I wasn't able to do for him and hold on to what I was able to do. It hurts me that he fell to the floor when he tried to get up in the few moments I left his room. I felt bad that there was something he wanted or needed, that he couldn't do, because he was so weak. I know He wouldn't want me to focus on these things. I know He loved me for taking care of him.

"Thank You for allowing me to lay beside him often during that long last day. Thank You that other people took care of the kids so I could focus on Zach. I thank You for an afternoon with him reading him the memory book he made for our family. Reading some of his favorite verses, quotes, and the poems he wrote was so special. Thanks for providing my sister Julie and my brother Jacob to help me sing *Amazing Grace* and *Blessed Assurance* to him.

"Zach kissed me several times when I got close to him and I feel so thankful to know that he loved me and wanted to communicate his love to me, even at the end. He made sounds throughout the day, but the only word I really understood toward the end was 'dream', when I was reading a poem he wrote about a dream. I am thankful that he seemed to be aware that Julie and Jacob were with us. It was a blessing that Ryan came to pray for him and read the Bible. Ryan said goodbye around 5:30 p.m. and told Zach he could go Home.

"After that, Zach didn't communicate much. I sat beside him on the bed. I kept talking to him about God, our family and life. Jacob started counting his breaths and we saw them getting slower. Toward the end, they got farther apart and sounded different. His last breaths were so far apart that I was surprised when the next one came. At 6:00 p.m., we said good-bye, after one final breath. My best friend on earth went to Heaven."

The hospice nurse arrived shortly thereafter and Jenny wrote: "Together, we prepared Zach's body so that family members could say good-bye before the funeral home staff came.

"I could have never imagined that my experiences caring for residents who died at the nursing home in my teens, was preparation for one last act of service for my husband. Family members came over and Zion and Moriah arrived.

"The three of us went into his room by ourselves so I could help them say good-bye. It was important to me that they saw Zach at home since he died at home. I didn't want them to come home and find Zach gone and not understand what happened. Zach and I had often told them that God would heal Zach in Heaven if He didn't heal him on Earth. Not sure what all I said to them in that moment but I know I told them that Zach didn't have cancer anymore and that he was happy with Jesus. I told them that the part of Daddy we love is in Heaven and that he didn't need his old sick body anymore."

~~~~~~~~~~~

ZACHARY L. BERTSCH, age 30, of Bluffton, Indiana passed away Thursday evening, June 6, 2013 at 6:00 p.m. at his residence, after a three year journey with cancer.

Worldwide data reveals 17 million people are diagnosed annually with cancer and 10 million people will die from it each year. Statistically, that equates to someone dying of cancer every three seconds, somewhere in the world.

At the beginning of this book we began Chapter One with the words – '*UNUSUAL? Yes! Zach Bertsch was unusual. Anyone who knew him would quickly agree.*'

Zach was only one of 10 million people in the world who died from cancer in 2013. As you read about his life, did you find it to be unusual?

In Chapter One I stated – "Zach would have been adamantly opposed to a biography written to bring honor to himself. But, if it could be used for God's glory, to enhance God's Kingdom, or to expose people to God, then he would have enthusiastically conceded and said with his cackling giggle, 'Let's do it'!"

After reading about Zach's life, did you pinpoint any situation where Zach took glory or praise for what happened in his life?

How many times did you see him pointing to God?

Was he an 'outlier'; someone standing out of the crowd?

Was cancer the winner?

Zach believed and practiced Revelation 4:11 throughout his converted life – 'Thou art worthy, O Lord, to receive glory and honor and power: for thou hast created all things, and for thy pleasure they are and were created'.

On Sunday morning, June 9, 2013, the Apostolic Christian church auditorium in Bluffton, Indiana was nearly full. The funeral service of Zach Bertsch was conducted as Jenny, Zion, Moriah, extended family, friends, co-workers and neighbors grieved his loss together, while simultaneously celebrating his life. His earthly battles, fatigue and pain were finished and Zach was laid to rest.

One of the last things Zach accomplished in his final week of life was to finish a letter he wanted read at his funeral. These were essentially his 'last words' to those he loved...

"Dear Friends and Family,

If you are reading or listening to this letter it means that I, Zach Bertsch, have gone Home to be with the Lord. My physical body is dead, but my soul is enjoying a grand entrance into the Kingdom prepared for those who love Jesus. It doesn't seem fair that you all have to go through a funeral and sadness while I get to enjoy happiness and celebration. Please find comfort in the fact that everyone who is born again in Christ will get their turn to enter eternal bliss and hear the King say 'well done'.

"Living with cancer for the last three years has been very difficult, but I have found incredible purpose in serving our Lord through this trial. As humans we long for purpose. I have met some people who were hopelessly depressed because they couldn't find purpose in their trials or in their lives. In fact everyone who doesn't follow Jesus lacks any real meaning in their life. If there is not another world that we enter after this life, then this life is without any purpose. I am so sad for those that I know who continue to live a meaningless life because they refuse to give control of their lives over to Jesus. They think that they have control of their lives, but ultimately they have no control and will suffer many consequences for their rejection of the Creator and the Redeemer of the world. Those who are unwilling to take a step of faith towards Christ take an even larger step of faith away from Him. I believe that it takes much greater faith to believe in nothing or not to settle on any particular belief than it does to believe in Christ.

"My greatest burden is still those who have not fully committed to loving and serving Jesus. There are some here who may view Jesus as an insurance policy, but have no true devotion which is shown by their lack of fruits. If you are not actively involved in a church, have not been baptized, or don't strive to keep His commandments then it is obvious that you are not a born again Christian. No one is saved by their works, but the lack of them in your life is evidence that you are not faithful to Christ. If you think that you are a Christian, why do other people doubt your salvation? If people have to wonder whether or not you are a Christian then you probably aren't born again. I would be thrilled if through my funeral service you come to a true relationship with Christ.

"The death of a human is no different than the death of an animal or a tree if Christ did not rise from the dead. I Corinthians Chapter 15 even tells us that we are of all men most miserable if in this life only we have hope. We find at the beginning of the same chapter in the Apostles' Creed that over 500 people saw the resurrected Jesus Christ. Many of them were willing to give their lives for Jesus, so this gives me tremendous hope that it is an historical fact that Jesus rose from the dead and therefore I too will rise again. I rest all of my hope on the fact that Jesus arose from the grave and that He will give me power to do the same thing.

"If we will rise again then this changes everything and I really mean everything. We will live our lives totally different if we think our lives are a small point in time before eternity begins. When we live with an eternal focus, we take every opportunity to serve Jesus, show our love to Him, and make sure other souls will also have a relationship with Him. If we don't believe any of this and this life is all there is, then we might as well make choices that fulfill our personal desires and show no regard for God's commandments. My prayer is that my life and death can convince some of you in this state to change your ways. It is not worth the risk that you are taking and you are missing out on the incredible joy, peace, and love that comes from serving Jesus. I so badly want to see you again in Heaven.

"The hardest thing about my battle with cancer has been the coming separation between me and my wife, Jenny, and the kids. I am very comforted by the fact that many people in the Body of Christ will stand in the gap as Christian friends for Jenny and as mentors for our children. The messages that I planned for my tombstone keep coming back to me as encouragements. On the front, the top verse says, 'For me to live is Christ and to die is gain'. - Philippians 3:7. The other quote on the front is: 'Only one life 'twill soon be past only what's done for Christ will last' - (C.T. Studd). When I dwell on the truth of these two statements I know that everything is okay. Making much of Christ is all that matters. The back of the tombstone has a picture of the Cancer Redemption Project on it with a quote from me saying, 'If God can use my cancer and my death to bring more souls to Jesus and give Christ more glory then it has been worth it all. God is good'. I am blessed to know that my cancer has been redeemed by God in a powerful way. I do not die wondering what the purpose of this illness is. I die knowing some of the great things that God had planned by allowing me to have cancer. I am convinced that the Cancer Redemption Project in Haiti will save many souls. I thank you all for your help for the project and Loving Shepherd Ministries for making it possible. Now that I am in Heaven I look forward to meeting many Haitian people who will be here because of God using my cancer for His glory. This means so much to me.

"My battle has been won and I am in a place of paradise beyond my wildest imagination, worshiping my Savior face to face. I look forward to some wonderful reunions as many of you join me in Heaven. Keep fighting the good fight. As A.W. Tozer said, 'The Christian need not fear death. The thing that Christians should fear very much is complacency'. I am so confident that the church body will hold the banner of Christ high until the end. Until we meet again soon. - In His Grip forever, Zach"

Two weeks after the funeral, Jenny wrote – "As I reflect on where our family is at right now, I can see how three years later (after Zach was diagnosed with cancer) the kids and I are starting on yet another journey. A journey without the husband and father we love. We have had two weeks to process our loss and I am guessing it will take months, maybe even years for us to fully understand how to cope with losing someone so important in our lives.

"Would I change what has happened to our family? I can honestly say 'no'. Of course, I wish Zach wouldn't have had to suffer so much. The pain in the moment was hard on him, but he always went back to the thought that he would gladly suffer if God would use his suffering to bring more souls to Jesus. I take comfort knowing that Zach died with no regrets."

If this were the end of the story, it would be phenomenal, but Zach's vision didn't end on June 6, 2013.

Chapter 18

July 9, 2013, I stood in front of 48 former orphaned, vulnerable and child-slave Haitian children and their new parents at the CRP campus. It had only been four weeks since Zach had gone to be with his Jesus.

I described to them the last days of Zach's life, his funeral and his love for each of them. One can only imagine what it's like to try to hold the attention of 48 children aged 4 - 12 years old. Right outside the open-walled pavilion where we met was a large soccer field with balls waiting to be kicked. It was 90° and we were sweating. But on this hot, humid, summer day, on a mountain top in southwest Haiti, all eyes were riveted, as everyone was anxious to hear more about Zach. He had become someone very special to each of them. Each knew the tragic backgrounds they'd been rescued from. They remembered the grief, loss and trauma surrounding them. They knew Zach's death had brought them life, hope and a new family.

The Cancer Redemption Project campus was nearing completion. The church and school construction was underway.

The first four Homes of Hope, Ezekiel, Abba, Mount Zion and Mount Moriah were flourishing. The fifth and sixth Homes of Hope, Daniel and Esther, would open in 2014 with 24 more children joining the other 48 kids at the CRP campus.

The children and parents watched silently and intently as I walked to the concrete north ledge of the large, open-sided fellowship pavilion. Looking out at the mountains and valleys, I pointed to the ledge and said – "When I was here in December of last year for the opening of the Zion and Moriah homes, Zach took me to this very spot and told me to sit down on this ledge. Sitting beside me, he looked me in the eyes, pointed up into the bright blue sky and said, 'Ed, I want to make sure you take good care of these families and children. If you don't, I want you to know that I'll be watching from up there'. Zach then laughed with his classic and memorable cackle, but I knew he was serious."

All the children at CRP know they are the *'chosen few'*. With a million highly vulnerable children in Haiti, the 72 who occupy the six homes know they are there because of Zach's cancer. Cancer didn't win. Cancer paid the price. God won and redeemed Zach's cancer.

They've become incredibly grateful as they grew to understand Zach had died so they could 'live'.

Though the children are extremely appreciative for a new family, the parents are just as honored and thankful to have a family. Since most were unable to have children biologically, they believe their prayers were miraculously answered when they received a dozen! They talk about how they are like Jesus with their twelve disciples!

As mentioned earlier, the concept of CRP didn't die on June 6, 2013. It was Zach's hope funding would continue to provide for yet more homes for orphans, vulnerable children and restaveks.

The names, 'Cancer Redemption Project' and 'CRP' became a source of confusion in Haiti, as some people thought all the children in the homes were suffering from cancer. So, a name change happened. The original campus became 'The Redemption Campus'.

Construction for two additional homes, the seventh and eighth, began in 2017, on a few more acres just across a small valley on another hillside. Now named 'Redemption West', it's less than 1,000 feet from the original campus. Those two new families attend the church and school at the Redemption Campus. That brought the total to eight Homes of Hope as children moved into the Redemption West campus on August 25, 2018.

Ninety-six children. All of them come from dire circumstances and were among the last, lost, least and lonely children of Haiti.

Pastor Wilfrid Remonvil, LSM's Director of the 20 Homes of Hope, speaks of the LSM and Redemption Campus children with a deep sadness. He was responsible for finding most of them and knows the circumstances from which they came. "Only God knows how many of these children would still be alive if they hadn't been brought from their miserable hometowns to a Godly family."

Abba Home of Hope

Ezekiel Home of Hope

Mount Moriah Home of Hope

Mount Zion Home of Hope

Esther Home of Hope

Daniel Home of Hope

Hosanna Home of Hope

Isabel Home of Hope

Occupying one-third of the church-school building, the church at the Redemption Campus opened on August 24, 2014. People from the surrounding countryside as well as from Redemption and Redemption West Campuses now call that church their 'home'. There have been many who have come to Christ over these first years. There have been baptisms, weddings and funerals and it's a vibrant church community as God has placed His hands on it.

The school on the second floor of the building at the Redemption Campus opened in October of 2014 and provides a quality education for many children. A large 'fellowship hall' area is in the lower level of the building below the school.

Another great use of the Redemption Campus has been its use for the LSM week-long Vacation Bible School for all LSM kids.

Zach had very lofty goals when he began the vision of the Redemption Campus Project. He desired the vision to be dynamic and ongoing, not having an end date. He was adamant that seven things would be accomplished:

Redemption Campus – Phase 1 - Though Zach didn't live long enough to see the Daniel and Esther Homes of Hope filled with 24 more children, he knew the fifth and sixth homes were under construction and would open in 2014.

Church and School – Again, though he wasn't able to see the church and school finished, he knew they would open within a year or so of his death.

Redemption Legacy Fund – Zach was adamant that funds would be set aside for the future sustainability of his vision. That was accomplished with the Redemption Legacy Fund to be used in the case of a funding emergency.

Family Sponsorship – Zach had a passion that others could participate in the Redemption Campus project by providing monthly support for the families. That program is in place permitting many U.S. families to walk alongside sponsored Haitian Redemption families by supporting the LSM Family Sponsorship Program.

Redemption Campus – Phase 2 – Zach said, "Not only do I want to see the Redemption Campus happen, I want the vision to continue to grow with other Homes of Hope and even more campuses." With the construction of the Redemption West Campus, Phase 2 is well underway and operating. Zach's desire was to see his cancer pay a price for caring for orphans in Haiti, again and again, long into the future.

Opportunities for Others – Zach was hopeful others diagnosed with cancer or other terminal illnesses would potentially catch the vision of using their personal trauma for God's glory.

Outreach – Zach was unwavering in his goal to use his cancer as a means of giving others the opportunity to come to Christ.

Redemption Campus   Redemption West Campus

CHILDREN in Loving Shepherd Ministries' Homes of Hope came from some of the most tragic and dire circumstances in Haiti. Though most were orphaned, some had become child-slaves or were on the verge of becoming child-slave restaveks. Some of the children are orphans due to the 2010 earthquake, the 2012 Hurricane Sandy storm, parents dying of AIDS, parental mental health issues and early parental death.

Jenny has a long history of working with vulnerable children. Her work as a Social Worker at Gateway Woods and as an Adoption Specialist at Loving Shepherd Ministries has given her many opportunities to work with foster children as well as families desiring domestic and international adoption. Those roles define 'who' she is.

Her and Zach's role as respite foster parents put her face to face with the needs of vulnerable children here in the U.S. All of that created a tender heart for what she, as a new single mom, Zion and Moriah were now facing since Zach was gone. After his death, she wrote –

"On June 12, 2010, my family's journey through cancer began when my husband Zach was diagnosed with stage IV colon cancer. Some would say that our journey ended with Zach's death on June 6, 2013. But for Zion, Moriah and me, the challenges related to cancer continue as we deal with the realities of our lives without a husband and father. Some days are really hard as we try to pick up the pieces and create a different 'normal'.

"When Zach passed away, we joined the ranks of countless women and children who aren't under the protection of a husband and father. But compared to most women around the world in this situation, I know we are blessed. Many women have no means of providing for the basic needs of their children, and their extended family members aren't able to help them because they are also experiencing great poverty.

"I have seen this firsthand in the lives of single mothers in Haiti. Their desperation and poverty often force them to give their children away to other families where they eventually become child-slaves (called *restaveks*). My heart hurts for these women and the hopelessness they feel. My heart also hurts for the many orphans in Haiti who desperately need a family to love them, care for their needs and raise them to be all God intends for them to be."

Jenny's words set the tone for this chapter as we look into the lives of specific LSM children and their background in an effort to paint a picture of the tragedies so many Haitian children face.

For privacy, the names of the children have been changed, but the circumstances and trauma which they came from are real. Each of the following children are now in an LSM Home of Hope.

Esther was brought to LSM by her sister in hopes that Esther would be able to be part of a Redemption Campus Home of Hope family. Her father had died before Esther was born and her mother was killed in the earthquake, leaving all seven children to care for themselves.

Rose was 10 years old when she was brought to an interview. Her mother had passed away and her father was an alcoholic. She didn't have a home and was continually passed from one family to another.

Marie came to her Home of Hope at 7 years old. Her father left the family long before and she had no memory of him. As the youngest of nine children in the family, she was considered the 'runt' and was often beaten by her sisters. Her family was involved in Voodoo and her grandfather cast a spell on her when she was very young. When she became part of a

Redemption Campus Home of Hope family, the demonic evidence of her past began to emerge. Fear, screaming, convulsions, kicking and flailing became a part of her nightly ritual. Prayers for Marie were often and fervent. Then, the outbursts suddenly stopped. LSM Pastor Wilfrid Remonvil contacted the remote grandfather and found that he had come to Christ at the same time the traumatic episodes stopped.

Judeline shared in her interview that she was 10 years old. Her mother had died and her father was a fisherman whom she rarely saw. She was living with her elderly grandmother and eight other people. It was feared Judeline was on the verge of becoming a restavek child-slave.

Lucie was 6 years old when she came to the Redemption Campus. She never knew her father, and her mother had abandoned her. Living with her grandmother was difficult because there was never enough money for food. Likely to become a restavek, she was lovingly accepted into a new family at the Redemption Campus.

Sophia was 6 years old when she was brought to an interview. She didn't know her father, and her mother had lost her mind. She went to live with her grandmother, but there were already six other children living with her. The grandmother was unable to care for Sophia, so she was brought to LSM.

Ella was 7 years old when her father died. It had been a long time since she'd seen her mother, so she lived with a cousin and eight other children. Times were desperate and the family often didn't have enough food to eat. Ella was at high risk of becoming a restavek.

Pierre at 5 years old was one of eight children. Both of his parents passed away, as did five of his siblings from cholera.

Pierre was being cared for by a distant relative, but obviously not well enough, as he had a large distended stomach from malnutrition.

Paul at 5 years old and his sister **Marie** at 3 years old were highly vulnerable. Their mother and father had passed away so they were given to an aunt who was physically challenged. Unable to provide for the children, they were brought to the Redemption Campus for an interview and then placed in a family.

Darlene's father died, leaving his wife and two year old daughter on their own. In October of 2012, Hurricane Sandy struck southwest Haiti. Darlene's mother started hemorrhaging during the storm and began walking on the road seeking help. She finally collapsed and died, leaving her daughter alone. Darlene was brought to the Redemption Campus for an interview and became part of a Home of Hope family.

Stephanie's mother passed away when she was very young. She was cared for by her non-working and sickly father. He finally gave up and forced the eleven year old out of the house. She was on her own, until a woman brought her to an LSM interview.

Cindy's mother and father passed away, so she became a restavek for a woman who was a Voodoo priestess. At 12 years old, she was forced to dance at the Saturday night Voodoo ceremonies. Finally brought to an interview, she became a part of a Home of Hope. She later said, "Before I came here, I had to dance for Voodoo. Now I can sing for Jesus!"

David's mother died when he was 7 years old. His father left when he was eight. For three years, he was a restavek to a woman who had her own children. David washed the family's clothing and dishes. He was responsible for walking to the river to get water for the family. The biological children didn't have any work or chores to do and David was often beaten for not working hard enough or fast enough. Finally at eleven he was given an opportunity to join a Home of Hope family.

Gerry's mother and father died from AIDS. He lived with his aunt and uncle, but when he became ill the couple forced him to live outside in their yard as they thought he had the same disease as his parents. Finally he was rescued from his desperate situation, found to be HIV Positive and placed in an LSM Home of Hope specializing in the care of children with HIV.

These are just a few typical stories of highly vulnerable children in Haiti who now live in an LSM Home of Hope. When they heard about the needs of these children, Zach and Jenny became passionate about sharing the stories and seeking funders to help. The LSM children are permanently placed with a Godly Haitian mom and dad who provide the most important resource to them – the Gospel.

Secondly, they are a part of a 'family'. In their new family, they receive the essentials relating to their physical, mental and emotional well-being. The care these children receive goes far beyond meeting their most basic needs. They are also provided valuable education related to critical thinking skills and given creative thinking opportunities so they can thrive in their culture, as those things aren't normally taught in Haitian schools.

Finally the children are given opportunities to process through their traumatic pasts in ways that will bring healing to their hearts and minds. This is essential in helping the children learn the skills they need to thrive as adults.

Loving Shepherd Ministries' mission statement is: 'Helping the world's most vulnerable children reach their God-given potential, so they can redeem their culture and country for Christ'. In short, a hopeless, helpless, vulnerable, orphaned, child-slave becoming a Godly country-changer.

Zach strongly believed God could bring orphaned and vulnerable children in Haiti from their helpless and hopeless situations to a place of great usefulness for Himself. Just as God brought him from a hopeless place with cancer, to a place of bringing glory, honor and praise to God.

Zach believed the more hopeless a situation is, the more God gets glory when the situation is miraculously changed.

The following statistics indicate the issues which perpetually drive Haiti's poverty and keep the country immersed in turmoil.

- 70% of the people have no meaningful employment.
- Though 60% of Haitian children begin school, only 13% of them will graduate.
- Of those who graduate from high school, 25% will be able to go to a Haitian university.
- Of those who graduate from a university, 83% will leave Haiti after graduation and seek employment abroad.
- Only 16% of Haitians are Protestant believers.
- Haiti is the poorest country in the western hemisphere.
- 24.7% of Haitians live on less than $1.25 per day. 59% live on less than $2.00 per day.

Many people talk about what God wants them to do. Zach spoke about those things, but he also lived them, as a testimony of how God wants to redeem each of our lives.

In their book *'Prepare to Die and Then Live'*, Zach and his brothers provided a 'devotion' for 'April 5' which perfectly mirrored Zach's passion.

'...and many wonders and signs were done by the apostles. – Acts 2:43b

Wow, how awesome is our God! The apostles were able to do many amazing miracles, signs and wonders. Souls were touched, hearts were pricked, and lives were changed. Thousands upon thousands were saved! If only we could be qualified enough to touch souls like the apostles did in the New Testament.

The simple truth is that you can! If you struggle with feeling unqualified or inappropriate to carry out what God has called you to do, just simply lay those burdens at the foot of the cross and offer everything you have to Him. Then, God can really use you to do wonderful and mighty works in His name just like He used the apostles. Remember, Paul was essentially a transformed tent-maker, Matthew was a transformed tax collector, Luke was a transformed physician, and many of the others were fishermen until they became transformed fishers of men. If these ordinary men can be totally transformed, we can too! God doesn't only call the Qualified; He also qualifies the Called.'

I think often about Paul's words to the church at Philippi – 'Being confident of this very thing: that He which hath begun a good work in you, will perform it until the day of Jesus Christ'. God isn't done with Zach's vision as we watch the ripples of the Redemption Campuses continue on and on until Jesus comes again.

Watching God work in Zach's life has been a reassurance of God's strength, peace and grace made available during times of trouble. Watching God redeem Zach, his cancer, the children in Haiti as well as redeeming each of us is likewise a powerful inspiration.

The word 'redeem' is defined as 'compensating for the faults or bad aspects of something. To gain or regain possession of something in exchange for payment'.

Zach and Jenny chose the word 'Redemption' for their project in Haiti. Zach was adamant his cancer would pay the price for God's

Kingdom work and unwaveringly stated that cancer wasn't going to win.

God, of course, knows all about 'redemption'. 'For God so loved the world, that He gave His only begotten Son, that whosoever believeth in Him, should not perish, but have everlasting life'. – John 3:16.

What greater miracle can we witness than to watch 'the last, lost, least and lonely' of this world be redeemed for Christ.

Zach's life can be an interesting 'read' or 'study'. Or, it can be a motivating factor in encouraging each of us to be pro-active in giving God permission to use our gifts, talents, time and resources for His Kingdom Work.

Zach often said, "'I can do all things through Christ which strengtheneth me', and 'my strength is made perfect in weakness', as he quoted Philippians 4:13 and 2 Corinthians 12:9.

We need not wait for a sickness, tragedy or failure to let God redeem it for good. He is able to redeem us now, as we are, in our weakness, with our failures, for His Kingdom work. He's waiting to hear from us.

Chapter 20

LIFE for Jenny, Zion and Moriah, after the loss of Zach continued, day by day, month by month, though there was a new normal gradually being created. The years of Zach's pain, suffering, death and resultant unknowns had taken a toll.

Others, of course, have been through the distress of losing a spouse, but the circumstances of each loss are very personal and unique. Jenny remembers her own private trauma over the next three years.

"The first two years after Zach died were really hard. In many ways they were harder than the three years we battled cancer. I filled pages and pages of prayer journals because that was the only way God felt real to me. I honestly don't want to reread those journals right now because I don't want to relive the pain contained in them.

"For a long time I felt like I was barely surviving. I felt pretty alone in my experience as a young widow because I had very few opportunities to interact with other women who had lost their husbands. During that time I watched as some close friends lost their son as well as seeing my sister lose her baby.

"My kids were hurting. They ended up in my room almost every night. Moriah had a lot of fears and separation anxiety. Zion expressed more anger and temper tantrums. Even though I am a pretty independent person I found it hard to make decisions at times. In addition to family, I was blessed to have a Christian counselor who walked beside me and helped me process all the hard things.

"In early July of 2014, one of my friends also lost her husband to cancer, so I walked through her grief with her and hopefully provided her the support I wished I would have had in that first year. This helped a lot, but also triggered memories of my first year without

Zach, because she experienced so many similar emotions and struggles.

"Then in the summer of 2015, two years after Zach's death, I traveled to Haiti with Zion, Moriah and other family members. It was a huge blessing to meet the new families in the Daniel and Esther homes as well as seeing the children from Ezekiel, Abba, Mount Zion and Mount Moriah again. Watching Moriah and Zion playing and having fun together with the 72 children from the six Redemption Homes of Hope was beyond comprehension. It was a dream come true. Missing in all of it was Zach and that brought emotions, but his heart, passion and vision were with us each step of the way. A lot of healing happened on that trip!"

"Over time, I learned to look back and see small progress toward healing. I also lived the reality that my dreams were still on hold. I researched about starting the adoption process as a single woman, but wasn't sure if I had the energy to care for another child. In the spring of 2016 I felt like Zion, Moriah and I were doing much better, so I started the process to become a foster parent. I stopped the process when I was introduced to Jordan Miller and we started talking about the possibility of a future together."

Zach had expressed multiple times about his desire for Jenny to remarry and have a new father on Earth for Zion and Moriah. That opportunity came on Moriah's 7th birthday, May, 15, 2016 when Jenny accepted Jordan Miller's proposal for marriage.

Engagement Day – May 15, 2016

She and Jordan were married on July 24, 2016. It was three years since Zach passed away, and now there was yet another opportunity to create a new norm.

Wedding Day – July 24, 2016 - (Pam Agler – *Moments...by Pam* – Credit)

On October 18, 2018, Jordan, Jenny, Zion and Moriah welcomed Titus Loren Miller into their family.

Though Jenny is busy with her family, her passion and heart is still strong for orphans, the vulnerable children of the world, foster children in the U.S., and for the Redemption Campuses in Haiti.

Jenny and Jordan became licensed Foster Parents in the summer of 2019 with the hope of using their home as a place of refuge and healing for hurting children.

With 140,000,000 orphans in the world [6]; 437,000 children in U.S. Foster Care [7]; and 125,000 children waiting for adoption from U.S. Foster Care [8], there will always be the need for people and families with passion and conviction to care for the 'fatherless' of this world.

Chapter 21

WHAT does God have in mind for the future with Zach and Jenny's vision for Haiti? As believers in Haiti often say, *'Sèl Bondieu ki konnen, men li kapab fè tout bagay!'* *(Only God knows, but He is able to do all things!)*

There is no question many people have been impacted by the vision God gave to Zach and Jenny for the Redemption Campus Project.

- 96 formerly orphaned, highly vulnerable and slave children have a Godly mom and dad and a lifetime family at the two Redemption Campuses.
- More importantly, the 96 children have been brought face to face with Jesus Christ and the Gospel, which is something that most likely would not have happened.
- Many unemployed Haitians have been given an opportunity to have Kingdom honoring employment. There's a common phrase in Haiti that states, 'For every person gaining meaningful employment, they are able to provide care for ten others'.
- Zach's selfless faith has encouraged many Haitians to have a different perspective of what an American Christian is.
- The church and school are a great outreach for sharing the Gospel of Jesus Christ.
- Zach's testimony of 'not letting cancer be the winner' inspired many people in the U.S. and spurred them to active engagement in Kingdom purposes.

Ephesians 3:20 says, '(God) who is able to do exceeding abundantly above all we ask or think, according to the power that worketh in us'.

This verse clearly establishes how such a great work as *The Cancer Redemption Campus Project* could have happened. It likewise defines what can happen when one man, full of cancer, decides to use it to glorify God.

Watching all that has transpired in Haiti because of Zach's vision appropriately expands our faith and our belief that God has more He wants to do.

So, what's next for Zach's vision?

- More Homes of Hope?
- More children rescued from the trauma of childhood slavery?
- Many more children brought into Godly families?
- Providing businesses, employment and supportive local church relationships so single mothers can keep their biological children with them?
- Reduction in vulnerable children becoming restaveks?
- More campuses?
- More illnesses, traumas and tragedies laid at God's feet, asking Him to use them for His glory?
- What visions are yet to be dreamed?
- What missions and ministries is God waiting to reveal?

As we think back to the first few chapters of this book, we learned several things:

1. We looked into the lives of 'successful' men and women and found that they were placed in a specific time, particular place and exposed to strategic people to accomplish great things.
2. If we study and believe God's Word, we find that successful people do not create their own success and are not self-made. They are used by God to help redeem a fallen world.
3. We've learned there is a 'God' who is orchestrating His Creation to accomplish His Will. He is our Omnipotent (all

powerful), Omnificent (powerful Creator of all things), Omnipresent (eternally present in all places at any given point of time) and Omniscient (all knowing) God of the universe, 'The LORD'.

Let's take one last look at the children who were, are and will be impacted by the vision God gave to Zach for 'Redemption Campuses'.

1. The children came from some of the most dire and tragic circumstances on Earth.
2. None of them chose their backgrounds and trauma.
3. None of them made an effort to be a part of a Redemption Campus Home of Hope.
4. Of the one million highly vulnerable children in Haiti, these specific children were chosen and uniquely set apart as future 'outliers' to become Godly country-changers in Haiti.
5. There was nothing special about the children that warranted their selection. In fact, they were among the most ragged, trauma-filled, poor, sickly and sad children of Haiti. They were the last, lost, least and lonely. _God_ put His hand on them and plucked them from their hard places for His Kingdom Purpose and began redeeming their painful pasts for His Glory.
6. The Haitian children have paralleled the lives of Joseph and Esther in the Bible. All were least likely to accomplish much, let alone be successful 'outliers'.

We have a clear mental image of who these children were and the tragedies they emerged from.

Without intervention and Jesus Christ we know what they would have become.

Now we are beginning to see glorious hints of their bright futures. Many have come to a personal relationship with Jesus Christ as born-again believers. They've already begun sharing the Gospel in their communities. They have tender hearts for the vulnerable children of Haiti. Some have begun their university and vocational educations as they prepare to be the next generation of country-changers.

Who are these children? They are the 'outliers' of Haiti. Young, undeserving and vulnerable children who were chosen and placed in a specific time, at a particular place and exposed to strategic people to be all God wants them to be... just like Joseph. Just like Esther. Just like Zach. Just like us?

Revelation 4:11 and Ephesians 3:20 – *'Thou art worthy, O Lord, to receive glory and honor and power; for Thou has created all things, and for Thy pleasure they are and were created'! – Because we know, You as God, are 'able to do exceeding abundantly above all we ask or think, according to the Power that worketh in us'!*

In Jesus' name, **Amen!**

APPENDIX

(1) *Outliers: The Story of Success:* by Malcolm Gladwell
Published by: Little, Brown and Company – Nov. 18, 2008

(2) *Wikipedia https://en.wikipedia.org/wiki/restavek* (Feb. 1, 2020)

(3) *The Proud Highway: Saga of a Desperate Southern Gentleman -*
by Hunter S. Thompson - Published by Ballantine Books – 1997

(4) *A Prayer of Weariness*: by Randy Alcorn
Poem originally published by Multnomah Press in 1986
in *'Women Under Stress'* by Randy and Nanci Alcorn.

(5) *Turn Your Eyes Upon Jesus*: by Helen H. Lemmel (1922)
© Warner Chappell Music, Inc., Capitol Christian Music Group

(6) *UNICEF – United Nations Children's Fund*
https://www.unicef.org/media/orphans

(7) *U.S. Dept. of Health and Human Services, Administration for Children and Families. Administration on Children, Youth and Families, Children's Bureau.*
https://www.acf.hhs.gov/sites/default/files/cb/afcarsreport26.pdf

(8) *U.S. Dept. of Health and Human Services, Administration for Children and Families. Administration on Children, Youth and Families, Children's Bureau.*
https://www.acf.hhs.gov/sites/default/files/cb/afcarsreport26.pdf